INFORMATION TECHNOLOGY
A Revolutionary Change

INFORMATION TECHNOLOGY
A Revolutionary Change
(In 9 Volumes)

Volume 4
(Evolution of Information and Communication Technologies)

Editor
RAMESH CHANDRA
Vice-Chancellor, Bundelkhand University, Jhansi (U.P.)

KALPAZ PUBLICATIONS
DELHI–110052

INFORMATION TECHNOLOGY: A REVOLUTIONARY CHANGE
(Information Technology)

Rs. 8000 (Set)
Rs. 900 (Each Volume)

ISBN: 81-7835-201-X (Set)
ISBN: 81-7835-223-0 (Vol. 4)

Published in 2003 in India by
Kalpaz Publications
C–30, Satyawati Nagar
Delhi–110052
E-mail: kalpaz@hotmail.com

Laser Typesetting at: Varsha Graphics, Delhi
Printed at: Mehra Offset Printers, New Delhi

Contents

Preface

The second half of the twentieth century has witnessed the global phenomenon of an information explosion. The development of different electronic technologies has made it possible for millions of people to have fast access to huge information resources stored in different places on the planet, to communicate with each other and to handle information presented in various forms. The Information and communication technologies (ICTs) pursue two main goals: processing information and transmitting information from one geographical point to another, from one person to another, to a group of people or to the whole community.

The singular technological feature, which is a turning point for ICTs, is the pre-eminence of the Internet Protocol (IP) for communication, around which ICTs are re-orienting and growing. This versatile connection-less protocol is a method by which data is sent over the Internet as packets from one computer to another, each having a unique address. Different packets may be delivered through different routes to their destination, where they are re-sequenced by the Transmission Control Protocol (TCP) and put back in the right order. The Wide

Area Networks (WAN) which are identified as Internet (international networks), Intranets (corporate or intra-organizational networks) and Extranets (extra-organizational networks) are all IP-based. IP has left its imprint not only on Metropolitan Area Networks (MAN) and Local Area Networks (LAN), but also on equipment such as the network computer, workstation, work group server, media server, Web server, cable TV networks, wireless 'last mile link' to the customer premises, set-top-box and even a kiosk.

With the whirling pace of change in communication technologies as we move toward an increasingly converged media environment, it remains vital to keep abreast of these developments. The digital media create unique opportunities to harness the power of technology as a positive force in the lives of people. However, the full potential of the digital media will not be realized unless there are clear public and private policies to help guide their development. In order to achieve this goal, we need a new framework for thinking about the media and their relationship to society.

Editor

1

Information Resources

The singular technological feature, which is a turning point for ICTs, is the pre-eminence of the Internet Protocol (IP) for communication, around which ICTs are reorienting and growing. This versatile connectionless protocol is a method by which data is sent over the Internet as packets from one computer to another, each having a unique address. Different packets may be delivered through different routes to their destination, where they are resequenced by the Transmission Control Protocol (TCP) and put back in the right order. The Wide Area Networks (WAN) which are identified as Internet (international networks), Intranets (corporate or intra-organizational networks) and Extranets (extra-organizational networks) are all IP-based. IP has left its imprint not only on Metropolitan Area Networks (MAN) and Local Area Networks (LAN), but also on equipment such as the network computer, workstation, work group server, media server, Web server, cable TV networks, wireless 'last mile link' to the customer premises, set-top-box and even a kiosk.

Hardware and Software Developments

Early computers were huge, expensive, complicated machines that consumed a lot of electricity, generated a lot of heat, needed specialist operators and were used for processing data in specialist laboratories. Their size, complexity and cost meant that they were not used for any library or information work until the mid-1960s, when transistors replaced the original valves. By then codes (such as the American Standard Code for Information Interchange or ASCII) had been developed so that text could be input, stored and output on these computers with the individual characters being translated into strings of binary digits.

Very large scale integration of the electronic components that comprise any computer has resulted in a huge increase in the power available and a decrease in the cost of processing. The 1980s saw the development of the microcomputer, which enabled many libraries and information units to acquire their own computer systems.

By the mid-1990s Personal Computers (PCs) have become commonplace in libraries and information units worldwide, and many people also have PCs at home. These PCs may be used for what has become known as 'edutainment', where educational packages which parents hope will improve their children's education are used, as well as encyclopedias on CD-ROM (such as Microsoft Encarta) and games, of which a large number are available.

With the development of the information superhighway many of these domestic PCs can now link to the Internet to access information sources that previously were only available in a library or information centre. Many professionals, including doctors, pharmacists, veterinary surgeons and lawyers, now have PCs on their desks. The battery-powered 'lap top' computer is a portable device that can be used when travelling on trains and planes. The hardware of a current PC comprises:

Central processor: The speed with which the processor carries out basic instructions (measured in millions of instructions per second (mips) or given as a frequency and measured in megahertz (MHz)) and the amount of main store that can be accessed are factors used to describe a processor.

The earliest computers processed up to 10,000 instructions per second and there has been continuous increase in this speed so that current PCs have a processing speed of thousands of mips. Intel is a major manufacturer of processors and in mid-1996 it announced plans for a 200 MHz Pentium processor which means that it will operate at two to three times the speed of current Pentiums.

RISC or Reduced Instruction Set Computer chips have been designed with the aim of speeding up the time taken to process an instruction by limiting the number of instructions to include those most often used. Another approach to improve speed is to have parallel processors so that the processor is not, as in most situations, processing a set of instructions one after another (or serially), but instead several processors obey instructions in parallel. Although the speed of processing has increased dramatically the cost of processors has decreased equally dramatically.

The main memory: The main memory of any computer is used to store information that is currently being processed. The earliest computers were capable of storing only 1,000 to 8,000 characters of information. The amount of store has increased continuously over the years with a parallel decrease in costs.

The most common form of memory can be written to as well as read from, and is referred to as RAM (Random Access Memory). The standard PC of today has a RAM of about 8, 16 or 32 MB (the unit normally used to refer to storage of one character is a byte; 1,000 bytes are called a Kilobyte or KB, and 1 million bytes are called a Megabyte or MB).

Input: A variety of input devices may be attached to a computer to enable information in any form (for example, text, voice, image) to be converted into the appropriate binary codes. The keyboard (many of which follow the QWERTY layout developed for typewriters in the late nineteenth century) is often the primary device for entering information.

The original ASCII code was seven bits long and capable of recognizing 128 separate symbols. This is not adequate for representing the range of symbols used in languages throughout the world. There are various other standards used. For instance the Arab Organization for Standardization and Metrology (ASMO) developed the ASMO 449 for Arabic characters, and the East Asian Character Code is based on work undertaken by the Research Libraries Group (RLG) in the United States for the processing of Chinese, Japanese and Korean ideographic characters. Unicode is the general name used to refer to the International Standards Organization (ISO) 10646 standard 16-bit code which encompasses the world's principal scripts and has been developed by a consortium involving computer manufacturers such as

IBM and Apple, and software developers such as Microsoft, as well as RLG and ISO.

A major input device of the 1990s has been the mouse, and its use to 'point and click' at sections of the screen is a common feature of current computer systems. Scanners can also be attached to PCs to input images or graphics.

Laser scanners are used to input the information from barcodes on books and borrower cards in circulation systems or from journal issues for serials control systems. Video scanners can be used as input devices so that a videoconference can be set up over linked PCs with the participants able to see each other, or for medical diagnoses. Touch-sensitive screens allow the user to point directly at, for instance, a particular option from a menu of possibilities displayed.

Storage devices: The traditional medium for storing data is based on magnetic materials. Most PCs have a hard disk which is in a sealed cartridge that contains the read/write heads. The capacity of hard disks has increased greatly over the years from about 5 MB in 1980 to as high as 2.5 GB in 1996 (a Gigabyte, or GB, is equal to 1,000 MB). Data can also be input and output on to floppy disk and most workstations have a floppy disk drive capable of reading and writing 3.5 inch diameter disks. Optical storage media have become increasingly popular in recent years and many PCs now have an integral CD-ROM reader. The price of CD-ROM technology has dropped dramatically over recent years owing mainly to the popularity of CD-ROM as the medium for games and entertainment products.

Output: The most common output device is the screen or monitor. Many monitors now do not just display text information but can also display the complex graphics and video that have appeared for games in the home computer market, and are also used in multimedia CD-ROMs. Speakers can be attached to deliver sound linked to images on the screen so that, for instance, Nelson Mandela's voice or the national anthem of Estonia can easily be heard when using Encarta.

Lap top computers use flat screens based on liquid-crystal display technology as this consumes little power. Hard copy printout is still required and there are now many high-quality laser printers available. Again the technology of printers has developed greatly and prices have decreased over the years.

The July 1996 issue of Personal Computer World published a comparison of what £1,500 would buy at various dates, showing the incredible developments in this area: 1979 Research Machines 380Z microcomputer with 16 KB RAM, tape interface and a second-hand teletype printer. 1983 BBC Microcomputer with disk filing and 800 KB store on two 5.25-inch floppy disks, a colour monitor and a dot-matrix printer. 1989 PC with 10 MHz processor, 640 KB RAM, graphics capability and a dot-matrix printer. 1992 386SX PC with 1 MB RAM, printer and Microsoft Works. 1993 486SX PC, 10 MHz processor, 8 MB RAM, 120 MB hard disk, Works for Windows. 1994 486DX PC, 33 MHz processor, 8 MB RAM, 424 MB hard disk, Works for Windows. 1995 486DX PC, 66 MHz processor, 8 MB RAM, 528 MB hard disk, multimedia capabilities with double-speed CD-ROM and sound card. 1996 Pentium PC, 75 MHz processor, 16 MB RAM, 1 GB hard disk, quad-speed CD-ROM drive, 17-inch monitor and modem (for Internet connection). Probably the major recent software development for library, information and archive work has been the use of the Windows interface.

In the mid-1980s an operating system known as PC-DOS (PC-Disk Operating System) was produced by the American firm Microsoft for IBM to use with its PC. At about the same time a completely different interface and operating system was developed for the Apple Macintosh computer; this made use of the point and click features of a mouse with different options displayed on the screen in the form of small pictures or icons. This type of interface became very popular with users and by 1990 Microsoft had developed a similar type of interface, known as the Windows 3 interface, for the IBM PC.

Microsoft has also developed a wide range of office support software that is used in many libraries, information units and archives. Examples include Word (for word processing), Access (for basic database management) and Excel.

Many archive and records offices use industry-standard software for their work. Simonson describes the use of general word processing and database management software (that is easily and cheaply available) for archive purposes at the Surrey Record Office in the United Kingdom. He notes that the advent of multimedia computing, networks and the information superhighway places the onus on archivists to find ways of making the information in their custody available electronically. There is also an urgent need for archivists to understand and get involved in the information revolution that is currently taking place, so that a coherent strategy can be developed for managing the electronic archives of the future. During 1995 Microsoft launched Windows 95, a 32-bit multi-tasking operating system, and this is now beginning to be used in libraries and information units worldwide.

Network Developments

This portion will provide a small flavour of how these developments impact on libraries and information units. When computers were first used in libraries it was often necessary to link terminals or workstations from remote branch libraries to the main computer system, or to link together various PCs so that they could, for instance, share a CD-ROM drive or a printer. These activities involved the implementation of some form of data communications network.

A network used to link equipment over a limited area is known as a local area network or LAN. In many universities around the world there are campus-wide LANs that enable students and staff from all over the campus to link to, amongst other things, the library's Online Public Access Catalogue (OPAC). Many libraries and information units have also become involved in providing access to a range of CD-ROMs via a LAN. There are many advantages to this approach:

> Several users may have concurrent access to the same CD-ROM. Library users may connect to a number of CD-ROMs from their own desktop PCs without having to handle the actual disc. Expenditure on CD-ROM licences may be reduced. CD-ROM discs and drives are protected from vandalism and theft.

—CD-ROM titles can be centrally updated.

There are various approaches to providing a CD-ROM network. The CD-ROMs can be attached to a network file server such as SCSI Express. Another approach is to use an optical server which is dedicated to running a group of CD-ROM drives. Products which provide this facility include CD-Net, CD-Manager and CD-Connection. A final approach, which is beginning to be popular, is to copy the CD-ROM data to magnetic disks. A major recent advancement in this area has been the development of products such as SilverPlatter's Electronic Reference Library (ERL), which provide the user with a seamless way of accessing CD-ROM databases, local databases and remote databases. CD-ROM has proved to be very useful in many countries. However, bibliographic databases on CD-ROM do provide users with information on items that may not be accessible locally and so the number of interlibrary loans rises significantly.

National or regional networks that link LANs or other computing facilities are known as wide area networks, the major one being the Internet. Often national libraries act as focal points in helping others in a particular country with this activity. The Conference of European National Libraries (CENL) is involved in the development of Gabriel -a World Wide Web server—which provides links to sources of information about the services and collections of members of CENL. It developed from work on Web servers carried out at the British Library (with its Portico server which, inter alia, provides access to images of treasures including the Magna Carta and the Beowulf Manuscript) and the Koninklijke Bibliotheek (KB) in the Netherlands (with its Alexicon service and the Hundred Highlights of the KB, recognized as a model virtual exhibition of a national library's treasures). The National Library of Malaysia is coordinating a project known as JARINGAN ILMU (or knowledge network) which involves many libraries in the country providing information for access on the

Internet. The Network of Networks project in Latin America, which is supported by the International Development Research Centre (IDRC), aims to improve the flow of information between eighteen networks in the region by the use of electronic mail, computer conferencing and the distribution of databases on CD-ROM.

The project started in 1993 and, as it developed, the possibilities of regional communication increased owing to the establishment of Internet nodes in places such as the University of Costa Rica and the University of Chile. Development of library housekeeping systems Library housekeeping (or management) systems typically are integrated packages which include modules for various cataloguing, OPAC, acquisitions, circulation, serials control and interlibrary lending. A detailed description of almost forty such library systems available in Europe is given by Leeves.

These systems include those that originate in one of the European countries and are available in others (for example, BIBDIA (Germany), LIBER (France), Pica (Netherlands), SuperMax (Denmark) and VUBIS (Belgium)), as well as those that are non-European in origin, mainly coming from North America (for example, ADVANCE from Canada and Dynix, Unicorn and VTLS from the United States). An overview of some twenty-seven companies involved in library housekeeping systems for North America, minicomputer based systems were sold by nineteen vendors, and sales in 1995 totalled 1,605 (as compared to 1,364 in 1994); the corresponding figures for microcomputer-based systems were ten vendors with sales in 1995 of 25,364 compared to 24,064 in 1994. The vendors selling most systems to academic libraries were Innovative Interfaces (INNOPAC), IME

(TINLIB), Ameritech (Dynix and Horizon) and Data Research Associates (DRA).

Great political changes have taken place in Eastern Europe during the 1990s and this has, amongst other things, opened the market for library systems. Developments related to library automation in Croatia, the Czech Republic, Hungary, Poland, Slovakia and Slovenia.

The Regional Library Programme of the Open Society Institute in Budapest, Hungary, was established in 1994 to support, promote and advance the information sciences in Central and Eastern Europe and the Commonwealth of Independent States, and has recommended long-term goals for automated access to library information. In order to support these goals a series of library automation workshops has been held in various countries of the region.

Some of the library housekeeping systems hold records in the Machine-Readable Records (MARC) format whilst others allow for the import and export of MARC-based records. There are a variety of MARC formats available and Campos et al. (1995) provide an overview of some of the national MARC formats (for example, CATMARC (Catalonia, Spain) and IndoMARC (Indonesia)) as well as the increasing use of the UNIMARC format. Countries that have adopted UNIMARC as a national standard include Croatia, Greece, India, Italy, Portugal and Slovenia.

The OPACs of many libraries worldwide can now be searched using the Internet. Some of these OPACs have been designed to be searched over the Web whereas others can be accessed using a Telnet connection. A special facility known as Hytelnet was developed in Saskatoon, Canada, and is designed to help users in searching OPACs at all Internet-accessible libraries via Telnet. Facilities are available to search by country and by system type, and to look at help files for searching the different OPAC types. Recent additions to the list of OPACs looked at during the writing of this chapter included those of: the National Library of Turkey (ALEPH), Shanghai (China) Jiao Tong University (in-house system), Universitat de Girona (Spain) (VTLS) and Universidad de Mexico (TINLIB).

The concept of an integrated library housekeeping package with the various modules accessing the same bibliographic record is beginning to be replaced by the concept of de-integration, with libraries buying different packages from different suppliers, and mixing and matching to best suit their particular needs. This has become possible because of various recent developments:

> The move away from the proprietary operating systems used by the integrated systems of the 1980s to open systems based on UNIX; examples include Geac's ADVANCE, Innovative Interfaces' INNOPAC, Fretwell Downing's OLIB, Sirsi's UNICORN and IME's TINLIB.

The move away from the proprietary database management systems to industry-standard relational database management systems. Examples include Geac PLUS's use of Informix, Dynix HORIZON's use of Sybase and OLIB's use of ORACLE. The use of client-server architecture in the design of systems. In the client-server model of computing a division is made between the applications software (which runs on a computer known as the client) and the database software (which runs on a computer known as the server). The two communicate with each other over a network using a communications protocol. Processing which involves data manipulation or screen display can be carried out on the client computer (thus reducing traffic on the network) and only database queries from the client and responses from the server need be communicated across the network.

The use of Z39.50: As defined by Dempsey et al. Z39.50 is a 'retrieval protocol which allows client programs to query databases on remote servers, to retrieve results and to carry out some other retrieval-related functions'. Its main impact on libraries is to enable users to search, say, the OPAC of a neighbouring library using the same OPAC interface as in their local library. For this to happen the local system must have a Z39.50 client and the remote system must have a Z39.50 server. Dempsey et al. list some of the library systems which incorporate Z39.50 client-servers; these include Geac ADVANCE, Dynix, INNOPAC, LIBERTAS, OLIB, Talis and UNICORN. Some of these clients are integrated with the standard OPAC (for example, LIBERTAS) while others are available as stand-alone products (for example, Dynix's WinPAC).

Networking developments: Library housekeeping systems no longer operate in a stand-alone fashion. Libraries which use a system to manage local processing of stock also need to provide their users with access to a range of information services as part of the electronic library; this could include access to networked CD-ROMs, locally loaded databases, the Internet and so on. Several suppliers now make information about their products and their company available on the World Wide Web.

The process of choosing an automated information system for libraries, museums and archives in the county of Suffolk in the United Kingdom. The chosen system provides traditional library management functions as well as access to networked CD-ROMs, local databases, the Internet and (for a trial period) access to OCLC FirstSearch databases. The factors influencing the choice of library software in sub-Saharan Africa. There, as in many other regions, good vendor support is an important factor as there is a marked absence of staff in libraries with relevant computer skills. Some software producers organize for local agents to supply the necessary training and maintenance functions of support. If local support for Western software is poor and/or very expensive there is an argument for the development of local software; examples include the SISPUKOM library management software developed within Malaysia and the INGRID system, based on Informix, developed at Tartu University Library in Estonia.

Library systems of the future will be very dependent on adhering to international standards. Work on standards forms part of the Open Interchange Initiative being carried out for the European Commission, and current information on a wide range of relevant standards for library and information work can be found on the Commission's web server. Developments in information retrieval systems A general overview of the developments in both local and remotely accessible information retrieval systems. Particular developments will be highlighted in this section.

Text retrieval software

For many years a range of software has been available

specifically aimed at information storage and retrieval of text-based information. Examples of such software include BRS/Search, CAIRS, CDS/ ISIS, Cardbox Plus, HeadFast, IdeaList and InMagic. CDS/ISIS is very widely used all over the world as it is available free of charge to non-profit organizations in UNESCO Member States and exists in a number of language versions. A regular feature on CDS/ISIS is included in Information Development. One recent example given of the use of CDS/ISIS is the DRAiN (Drainage Information System) project which aims to co-ordinate information from various relevant research organizations in Egypt, France, India, Mexico, Pakistan and Uzbekistan involved in irrigation and drainage research.

For many years text-retrieval software was used to process bibliographic data, but recent developments in storage technologies have meant that this software can now be used also for full-text retrieval purposes. The producers of this software have continued to develop their products and many now run under Windows, can deal with graphical data as well as text data and can be used when creating local CD-ROMs. A special category of text-retrieval software is personal bibliographic software (such as Pro-Cite, Reference Manager and EndNote Plus) which may be used by academic researchers and which offers pre-defined data structures and pre-defined output structures (to comply with bibliographic styles adopted by organizations such as the American National Standards Institute (ANSI)) as well as standard facilities such as Boolean searching and batch importing of records.

An introductory essay by David Bearman (1994) in a directory of about eighty software packages for use in archives and museums notes that the 'problem with archives software has historically been that the market is too small and diffuse to support a range of products'. However, he points out that the Internet provides an exciting domain for archivists with the possibility of setting up World Wide Web servers of archives holdings which might include images and sound information as well as document delivery services (for example, British Columbia Archives and Record service. Geographic information systems (GIS) GIS software comprises tools for the collection, analysis, retrieval and display of spatial information.

Technologies that integrate the management and analysis of this type of data (from maps, weather satellites and so on) are being used in a variety of ways for environmental studies, global change research, transportation planning, urban planning, marine studies, and so on. As with bibliographic data, there is a need to share resources worldwide and the MARC format is being investigated as one possible solution. One of the projects - Project Alexandria (not to be confused with the plan for the new library of the same name at Alexandria in Egypt) - being funded in the United States as part of the National Science Foundation (NSF) digital libraries programme, is developing a system to access spatial data in distributed databases. A number of papers on GIS is included in Information Technology and Libraries, June 1995.

Traditionally the information that can be stored and retrieved in computer systems used for library and information work has been structured into databases. The growth of databases has been rapid. A database as a collection of data or a body of information that is organized for retrieval via a computer in any storage medium', and they cover databases that may be online directly from the producer, through a third-party online service or in CD-ROM format. The types of information covered in these databases include:

> Bibliographic data relating to articles published in the primary journals: MEDLINE (medical), Compendex (engineering), LISA (librarianship), Inspec (electrical engineering and computer science).

Details from the book trade (BookBank, BNB, BookFind, Books in Print). Full-text information such as newspapers (The Times, the Guardian, the Independent), articles from specialist journals (ADONIS - Biomedical, BPO (Business Periodicals Online), New Scientist), literature (English Poetry) and patents (US Patents FullText).

Multimedia products (McGraw Hill's Encyclopaedia of Mammalian Biology, Hulton Deutsch CD Collection, Encarta, Cinemania). There is a wide range of organizations involved in publishing databases; these include traditional academic publishers (Oxford University Press, Elsevier), learned societies (Institute of Physics, Institute of Electrical Engineers), commercial companies (Institute for Scientific Information, Derwent), the computer industry (Microsoft) and the entertainment industry (Sega, Disney, Nintendo). Work on quality issues of publicly available databases has been undertaken by various online user groups, and Armstrong describes the concept of 'database labelling', which would provide the potential user with basic information about the database and the extent to which the information contained could be trusted.

As well as the traditional online search services (such as Dialog, DataStar, STN and ESA-IRS) there are now many others ways in which libraries and information centres provide access to publicly available databases for their users. Examples include stand-alone and networked CD-ROMs, locally mounted databases and Internet access. The online search services provide access to a range of databases. Many of the early databases were bibliographic and dealt with scientific and technical information.

During the 1980s more specialist services appeared and the existing services broadened their scope. FT Profile, for instance, specializes in the provision of full-text online information tailored for the business community. OCLC entered the online search service field in late 1991 with FirstSearch, a service designed particularly for end-users. In the United Kingdom the Joint Information Systems Committee (JISC) of the funding bodies for higher education has organized the establishment of centralized databases for the academic community. By charging a university a fixed annual fee, searching becomes 'free at point of use' for researchers, teaching staff and students.

The rise in the use of the Internet has been accompanied by the development of commercial, consumer-oriented online services. Examples include America Online, Prodigy, Compuserve, Genie and Delphi which are popular with end-users as they cover a range of information such as news, general health matters, encyclopedias, business information and magazines.

CAS-IAS provide access to the table of contents of several thousand current journals and also provide means of transmitting requested articles. By making use of CAS-IAS services some libraries are moving from a just-in-case mode of operation with respect to serials holdings to a just-in-time mode. Examples of CAS-IAS include OCLC FirstSearch (with the Article 1st and Contents 1st databases), UnCover (now owned by Knight-Ridder, which also owns Dialog and DataStar) and Inside Information (from the British Library).

Interface Developments

The early online search systems such as Dialog, DataStar and ESA-IRS relied heavily on command languages for carrying out online searches, and this helps to explain why these systems were mainly searched by specially trained intermediaries. With the developments of OPACs and CD-ROMs in the 1980s, an interface was needed which could be fairly intuitive with searchers and needed no special training. The technique adopted was to provide the searcher with a menu of options on the screen so that an appropriate option could be selected which would then lead to another set of options or to the data. On the positive side, menus can be self-explanatory, easy for the novice searcher and give a structure to the search. However, they may be slow to work through and irritating for frequent searchers.

With the major move to a Windows environment, many producers of search systems are developing their software to work in Graphical User Interface (GUI) mode. When a screen of potentially clickable items is presented it is not always obvious to the novice searcher where to go next in this two-dimensional environment and so there are many aspects of screen design that need to be borne in mind by the interface developer. Eight golden rules for any designer of a search interface. Paraphrased these are: strive for consistency, enable frequent users to take shortcuts, offer informative feedback, give action sequences a logical structure, offer simple error handling, permit easy reversal of actions taken, make the user feel in control and reduce short-term memory load.

Retrieval techniques

Most retrieval software is based on the user combining chosen terms or phrases using the standard Boolean operators AND, OR, NOT in the search statement. Over the years various alternative techniques have been developed by researchers; these are referred to in the literature as best match, nearest neighbour, probabilistic retrieval, fuzzy sets, relevance ranking or ranked output. Some of these ideas are now appearing in commercial services such as Personal Library Software's Personal Librarian, Dialog's TARGET, and FREESTYLE developed for the LEXIS legal service and the NEXIS news service. Evaluating the performance of various information retrieval systems has been a topic of interest for many researchers over the years. A major initiative, known as the Text Retrieval Conference (TREC), involves a number of research groups from around the world testing their information retrieval techniques on the same databases of full-text items.

Human aspects of automation

There are many potential problems related to the use of information technology in archive, library and information work, and these can result in useless, expensive and inappropriate systems. There have been examples of libraries where much time, effort and money is spent on the latest software and hardware but little time has been spent on revising work practices or ensuring that workstations are ergonomically designed for the people who use them.

Only about 10% of the literature on library automation covers human aspects, whereas about 80% of the problems that arise in automation projects are thought to be caused by human or organizational matters. It is most important to consider people at all levels when setting up any form of computer system in a library. The real needs of the users must be taken into account in the design; library staff and computer staff need to know enough about each others' areas of expertise so that they can communicate properly; systems librarians and network managers need to have suitable job descriptions so that they do not become too 'techno-stressed'; workstations need to be suitably designed for their likely users; users need to have realistic expectations of the new system; and library staff need to be kept informed in an appropriate way.

Traditional organization structures may need to be adapted with the introduction of new systems. In many countries where legislation is in place to cover the health and safety aspects of, say, working with VDU (Visual Display Unit) screens, managers are being forced to think about the human aspects of automation. There is much to be done in making sure that human factors are considered at all stages in the design of a computer system for use in libraries or information units. The impact on people of electronic libraries (IMPEL) is one of the supporting studies to the e-Lib project.

All librarians and information workers must be able to cope with the vast quantity of electronic information now available as well as to advise their users how to cope with it.

The use of information technology in libraries in the Philippines, and notes that problems are due to lack of know-how, lack of direction, lack of funds and a weak telecommunication infrastructure. The first three reasons could be applied to many libraries all over the world.

Some manufacturers make their products available on the world market and have invested efforts in translating the interface dialogue of their systems into various languages. TINLIB, for instance, is available in about twenty-five different languages and is used in libraries on five continents.

ALEPH, from Israel, can handle several different scripts (including Arabic and Hebrew) within a single record and has been used in many East European countries, including the Czech Republic, Hungary, Slovakia and Romania.

There are, though, few examples of truly multilingual systems for information retrieval; the Institut Textile de France developed a system (TITUS) which enabled searchers to search, in say German, for a document which might have been input in Spanish; the Swiss Federal Institute of Technology in Zurich has developed ETHICS; and in Malaysia, SISDOM is a retrieval system which deals with documents in Malay and English. The madness of technolust and describe how 'effective users of electronic resources must learn to surf the networks, and on occasion, to swim in information without drowning in data'.

Multi-media Technologies

During the last decade, there have been endless and dramatic technological changes in all three major areas of information technology computing, communications and content. We have witnessed the advent of personal computers, worldwide packet networks, optical disk and other mass storage media, interactive video technology, image technology, digitizing and scanning technology, computer graphic technology, and the growth in both size and number of massive public and private databases - bibliographic first, then numeric, and now multimedia. These three major areas were rather disparate in earlier years. Now, they are becoming integrated and quite international in scope and impact. There is every reason to believe that this situation will continue at an even faster pace. Now, the world is going digital, and there is no turning back.

The concept of mixed media or multimedia has been around for some time, the form and its impact having been registered well before the advent of the computer, personal or otherwise. Though many people even today think of the computer mainly as a number-cruncher, early visionaries like Vannevar Bush already saw its future role as an information and media processing powerhouse in the 1940s. In his famous 'As We May Think', published in the July 1945 issue of Atlantic Monthly, Bush advocated mechanizing scientific literature by association with a device called 'memex'.

Bush's idea endured and inspired two people about twenty years later—Douglas C. Englebart of the Stanford Research Institute and Ted Nelson of Xanadu. Englebart, influenced by Bush's vision, developed a system for knowledge workers, called NLS (oNLine System) in 1963, which embodied many original ideas and concepts of hypertext, including windows, the mouse, electronic mail, and a hypertext-like ability to link and annotate documents. Nelson coined the word 'hypertext' in the 1960s, which he described as non-sequential reading and writing that links different nodes of the text.

Hypertext and hypermedia/multimedia

Hypertext mimics the brain's ability to access information quickly and intuitively by reference. At the basic level, a hypertext system is a database management system which permits one to connect screens of information using associative links, and by allowing users to link information together, thereby creating trails through associated materials.

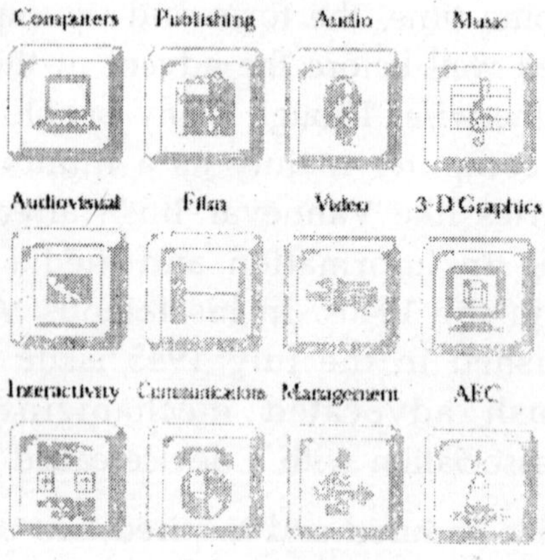

Figure 1: Hypermedia Map

At the more sophisticated level, a hypertext system has a software environment which supports collaborative work, communication and knowledge acquisition. When the system's database structure is complex, it is common to supply a special node called a graphical browser which displays the structure of the database and serves to re-orient users who are dislocated. Hypertext is the forerunner of multimedia/ hypermedia. Although the concept of hypertext has been with us since the 1940s, it was brought down to the 'household' level only after the introduction of Apple's HyperCard in late 1987. Using HyperCard, one can create links in a given work—an electronic book, multimedia presentation or anything that might best be explored in a non-linear way. Then, when users are reading or exploring, they can click on icons to zoom to related topics which may be in the same file or in another one.

Hypermedia extend the hypertext concept to link textual material to all forms of material—graphics, image, video, animation and sound—that may bedigitally encoded for storage and retrieval through computer-based systems. As early as 1988, Casa-Bianca, in his attempt to publish a hypertext-like journal, Hyper-Media, graphically presents a typological framework of hypermedia in what he calls HyperMedia Map. He uses graphic icons, as shown in Figure 1, to illustrate how the world's communications media - audio, audiovisual, film, music, video - have been incorporated with computers, communication networks, publishing and information resources, 3-D graphics, design and system management to enable us to provide multimedia/ hypermedia information in a new, global, 'wired society'.

Clearly, multimedia technologies are not one single technology, and there is no single product, or definable market. The term 'multimedia technologies' epitomizes technology integration through the use of multimedia tools. In order to summarize the above and facilitate our discussion on multimedia, a simple working definition of multimedia is proposed as follows.

Multimedia extends the hypertext concept of non-linear and non-sequential links of textual material to all forms of material that may be digitally encoded for storage and retrieval through computer-based systems, including images, sound, graphics and animation . . . Thus, multimedia refers to a synthesis of text, data, graphics, animation, optical storage, image processing and sound. Clearly, multimedia technology is not a single technology, and there is no single product, or definable market. It epitomizes technology integration.

Multimedia tools and technology Input and output technologies: hardware and software for digital data, sound, image, video and films As librarians and libraries everywhere are still handling largely printed materials, it is important to understand that the information seekers are no longer satisfied with only printed materials. They will want to supplement the printed information with more dynamic sound, music, graphics, animation, photography and video, all of which can now be fed into an ordinary computer where they can be cut, changed, shaped, combined, manipulated, enhanced and reconstructed into all kinds of exciting information products. In order to benefit from the current multimedia environment, one needs to know the multimedia tools available in the marketplace so that they can be used to bring multimedia to the desktop.

Hardware and software for users of multimedia

Currently the marketplace is full of multimedia products, as shown by the thousands of titles included in any directory of multimedia titles, many of which are multimedia CD-ROM titles. For libraries' interest, multimedia products of every reference type, as well as subject topics, are available. Because more and more products have incorporated rather large numbers of images, sound and digital videos, much more powerful hardware than the bare minimum requirement for a PC system will be required:

— 80386 CPU.

— EGA/VGA or VGA A Plus Graphics.

— 2 MB RAM.

— Double-speed CD-ROM Drive.

— Microsoft Windows 3.1.

The general rule is that whenever possible, try to acquire a system with as much speed, hard disk space and RAM as possible. For example, some products will run properly only with a 486 or Pentium processor with at least 16 MB of RAM and a four-speed CD-ROM drive. The unfortunate fact is that most multimedia application products are developed for users with the higher-end systems, and few have kept the low-end systems users in mind.

Multimedia production tools

Only a couple of years ago, producing multimedia applications was generally difficult, since most multimedia production tools were either not readily available or simply too expensive for general use. But fast technological development has made it possible for many to consider producing their own multimedia applications now. To facilitate librarians' use of these tools for production purposes, those for both Macintosh and PC systems are included below. Although Macintosh tools are often preferred for the development of multimedia applications, they might not be readily available to libraries in developing and less developed countries.

There are simply too many multimedia production tools to cover all adequately. For example, for the Macintosh platform alone, the Macintosh Multimedia & Product Registry lists on forty-five pages over 700 tools in every possible category of production work.

A similar publication including tools for the PC platform is IBM's yearly issue, Multimedia Today: The Sourcebook for Multimedia. The issue for 1995 lists over 600 production tools. For illustrative purposes, the following discussion covers only a very small number of selective tools in some distinctive categories.

Animation

The best known animation tool is Macromedia's Director 4.0 (H) which is available for both Mac and Windows. Macromedia's Director is a powerful animation and authoring tool. Users can create, combine and synchronize graphics, text and animation with audio and video; add full interactively with buttons and scripts; export and import QuickTime movies, etc.

Conversion software is also available to convert Mac Director applications to PC and vice versa. Other notable software includes Adobe's Premier 4.1 (H), Avid's VideoShop 3.0 (M) for Mac, and Gold Disk's Animation Works Interactive 2.0 (L) for PC.

Clip art and photography

In this category, Photo-CD technology has been utilized fully by most producers to store about 100 images of clip art and photographs on almost every subject for both Mac and PC platforms (some store 600 when the top two levels of higher-resolution images are sacrificed). Of international interest, Educorp's International Graphics Library is a CD with 32-bit QuickDraw images (L). These clip art images can be copied and pasted on multimedia applications. More clip art CDs can be found in various software catalogues from Image Club in Milwaukee.

Development tools

The marketplaces has over fifty development tools for multimedia authoring and digital publishing. For Macintosh, the most noteworthy is HyperCard (L) (current version is 2.3). It features an intuitive interface designed to guide users through the construction of hypermedia programs and presentations of various media elements such as pictures, paint graphics, QuickTime movies, audio, videodisk sequences and text, where users want them simply and quickly. Other popular ones include Macromedia's Author-ware 3.0 (H) for both Mac and Windows, the Voyager Co.'s Expanded Book Toolkit (L) and SuperCard 3.0 (M). Other PC systems include Aim Tech's Icon Author (H) and Motion Works' Media-Shop (M) and ToolBook (M).

Most noteworthy in the drawing and painting category are Adobe Illustrator 5.5 (M), Canvas 3.5 (M), Macromedia's Freehand 5.0 (M), Claris' MacPaint 2.0 (M), and Adobe's SuperPaint 3.5 (M). All are powerful illustration and design tools that simplify the creation, manipulation and refinement of artwork with advanced features for editing, text handling, colour support and more.

Image processing

(Photoshop 3.0.3 for Mac) is the most recognized and most powerful image processing tool. It lets users design artwork with a wealth of powerful painting and selection tools, or retouch and correct true colour or black and white scanned images with image editing tools and filters. It also has a wide range of third-party plug-ins for enhanced image manipulation, most notably Kai's Power Tools 2.1 (L), which provides a set of three dozen powerful extension and filter plug-ins that expand the ability to create computer-generated artwork and manipulate scanned images. Aldus PhotoStyler 2.0 (M) for Windows is also a popular tool for PCs.

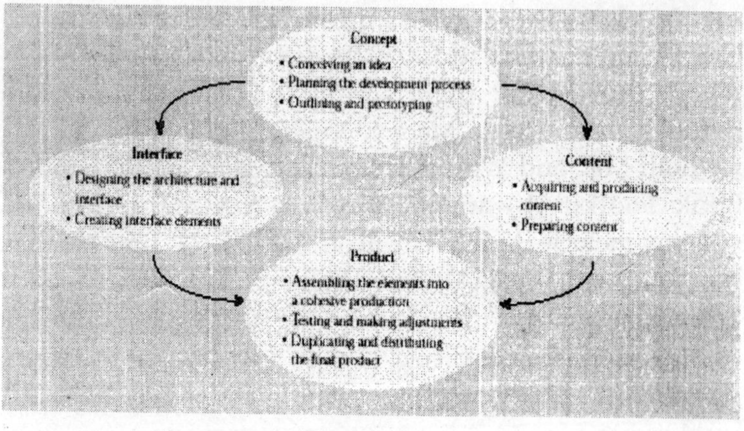

Figure 2: Basic Steps in Developing multimedia applications

Media catalogues

A number of tools are available for organizing and quickly retrieving digital photos in categories. Adobe's Fetch 1.2 (L), In space System's Kudo ImageBrowser (L) and Kodak's Showbox (L) fall into this category for Mac, while Electronic Imagery's Image-Manager (L) and Lenel Systems' Media Organizer (L) are for PC users.

Modelling and rendering

Numerous powerful tools are available in the marketplace for creating photo-realistic computer images and animation at an affordable price (under US$1,000) for the type of sophisticated work that was possible only with mainframe and minicomputers a few years ago. Some powerful tools are Specular International's Infini-D 3.0 (M), Strata Inc's Strata Virtual (L) for real-time renderer, Macro-media's Swivel 3D Professional 2.0.4 (M) and Virtus Corp.'s Virtus VR (L). Tools from Strata and Virtus are for both Mac and PC systems.

Music software

Music is an important element of a multimedia production. Various tools are available as a MIDI (Musical Interface for Digital Instruments) sequencer, editor and performance tool that provides multitrack recording, precise editing of all musical events, etc. These include Unicorn's Performer 5.02(M) and Opcode Systems' Vision 2.0 (M) for Mac, Midisoft's Studio (M) for Windows and Turtle Beach System's Wave for Windows (M) for PCs. Digi-Design's SoundTool (M) consists of a sound accelerator card and Sound Designer II (software) which allow hours of CD-quality sound to be recorded on to a hard drive and edited with unparalleled precision.

Optical character recognition

For multimedia applications, there is a great need for text materials as well. Thus, it is important to have effective tools to be able to turn hard-copy printed texts into digital word-processing files. Optical character recognition (OCR) software is very useful for this process. An outstanding example is Caere's OmniPage Professional (M), which is an advanced OCR solution to turn printed texts into word processing files. It is available for both Mac and PC. Another competitive OCR software for Windows is Xerox's TextBridge Pro 96 (M).

Presentation and video-editing software. Many high-powered software tools are available foron-screen animation presentations with motion, sound and QuickTime, and flexible non-linear editing systems for Mac. For presentation purposes, Gold Disk's Astound and Adobe's Persuasion 3.0(M) are powerful graphic and digital video software that will produce or deliver data-intensive multimedia presentations. Macromedia's Director 4.0 (H), Adobe's Premier 4.1 (H), and Avid's VideoShop 3.0(M) are powerful tools providing an economic means of professional video editing. Director and Premier are available for both Mac and PC systems. Other PC desktop presentations include Motion Works CameraMan (L), Eduquest's Linkway 2.01 (L) and Linkway Live! (L), Lenel Systems' MultiMedia Works (L), and IBM's Storyboard Live! 2.0 (L).

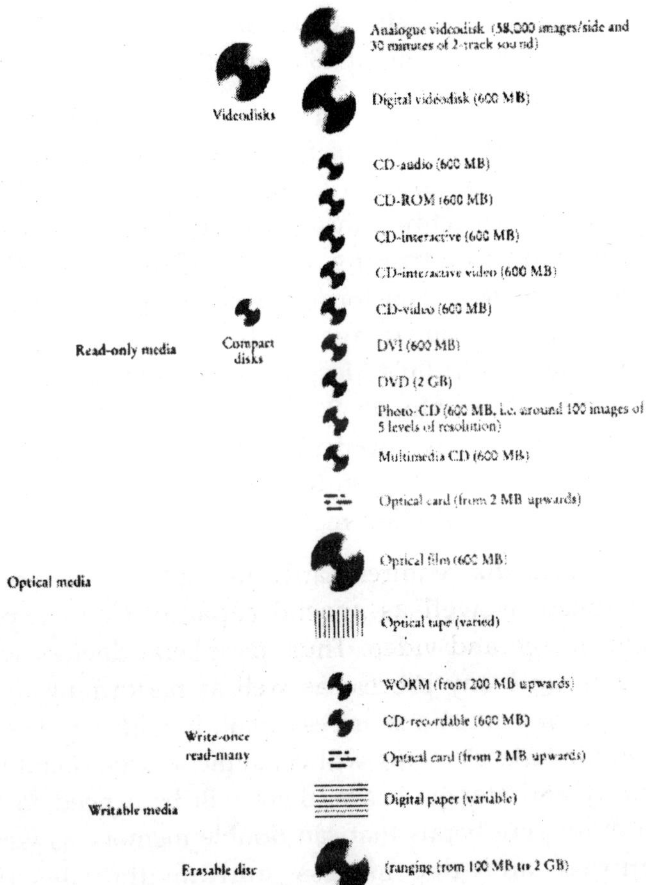

Figure 3: Types of optical media

Special effects

Like clip art and photographs for fast and easy use of still images, there are many clip media products available for immediate use of ready digital videos, such as Macromedia's ClipMedia˙ (M) with professional animation, sounds and videos arranged on CD-ROMs in various subject categories (education, business, medicine, etc.). Many products, like Olduvai Corp's Sound Clips 1.0 (L), feature an average of 100 sounds per volume.

In addition, software tools are available for producing special effects for multimedia production. One of the most used is Gryphon's Morph 2.5 (L) for Mac, which smoothly transforms one image into another with dynamic morphing. Gallery Effect 1.51 (M) is another tool that transforms scanned photographs and other bit-mapped images into works of art. The counterpart of Griffin's Morph (L) for PC is North Coast Software's PhotoMorph 2 (L), which allows users to combine and apply sophisticated special effects to bit-map images and AVI video clips, with features for desktop video, including motion morphing.

Multimedia requires hardware and software power and speed as well as special capabilities to capture sound, image and video. Thus, peripheral devices which can accelerate any process as well as performing any of the capturing functions are essential. In addition, because all multimedia elements will consume a large quantity of memory and storage space, there will be a need to look into those peripherals that can double memory as well as compress and decompress multimedia files. The following are samples of peripherals which are worthy of serious consideration.

Accelerators

Many accelerators and chargers, such as DayStarDigital's Image 040 (H), can accelerate imaging functionsup to 600%. Unfortunately these boards are generally quite expensive (over US$1,000) and are intended for high-end operations.

Audio/video controllers

IBM's M-Motion Video Adapter/A (H) for PS/2 can receive and process analogue signals from multiple external video and audio sources, and then send them to a monitor and external speakers for immediate viewing/listening in multimedia application settings. In this way, a PC can be connected directly to an analogue videodisk device and grab the analogue videos directly to integrate into multimedia applications. The Creative Labs' Sound Blaster 16 boards for PCs provide rich CD-quality stereo sound for multimedia, education, business, home and entertainment applications at affordable prices.

Digital cameras

In the last two years, several reasonably priced high-performance digital cameras have been introduced. Apple, Canon, Kodak and others have produced such digital image capture devices at a cost ranging from $350 to over $1,000. Users should acquire cameras only after studying carefully their need for digital images. These digital cameras can be connected to hardware systems using any platform. Most digital cameras function like regular cameras and therefore are mainly for capturing individual images. Another type of digital camera which can capture both colour pictures and videos is becoming quite popular. Examples include VideoLab's FlexCam (L) and Connectix's QuickCam (L). These are compatible with all leading video digitizing boards. Each is an integrated colour camera and microphone and can produce video output in both NTSC and PAL.

In addition to software, built-in hardware capabilities or addition digitizers and frame grabbers (generally these are additional peripheral boards) are required for real-time digitizing of sound, images and video. For example, Macromedia's MacRecorder Sound System (previously marketed by Farallon) includes both the digital sound recorder hardware and SoundEdit software for users to record, edit and play back live or prerecorded sounds on a Macintosh. Digital frame and video grabbers are abundant in the marketplace. For example, Radius' SpigotPower AV (M) provides full-screen, full-motion capture and playback of interlaced and non-interlaced JPEG video. It is able to capture and save full 24-bit colour data. Creative Labs' Video Blaster boards of different models can bring full-motion video sequences to a PC. Users can capture analogue video sequences at up to thirty frames per second. Generally one connects the television video recorder, and/or video camera to these boards.

Scanners

Scanners are essential for turning hard-copy texts, pictures in both positive and negative forms and films into digital files. Because of these different original formats, there are also different types of scanners. These include:

> Flat-bed scanners, such as Microtek's ScanMaker II (M) and III (H) models, that convert printed and artwork to digital files. For example, the ScanMaker III (H) is a 36-bit colour high-resolution flat-bed scanner up to 1,200 dpi. Generally, a scanner with at least 300 dpi can be quite effective for multimedia application development. Although more expensive and higher resolution drum scanners are also available, they are generally too expensive (some are over $35,000) for general-purpose use.

Slide scanners that will do the same with photographs, such as Microtek's ScanMaker 1850S (M). Film scanners, such as Microtek's ScanMaker 35t (H), that can scan any 35 mm slide in 24-bit colour mode in up to 16.7 million colours or in 8-bit grey-scale mode to capture up to 256 shades of grey.

Hand-held scanners (L) that generally provide a low-cost alternative for producing digital images for multimedia applications. However, the resolution of these scanned images is low and the images can easily be distorted. Need for mass storage in information work (archives, library and information services)

Library, information and archival work generally deals with very large quantities of information. Regardless of whether information sources are in printed or electronic formats, space is always a key issue. Mass storage is required to meet:

— The need for a large-volume digital storage system for archival management.

— The need to provide users with immediate access to the rapidly growing volume of data and information that is stored in digital information systems and is likely to be distributed on optical media in the future.

— The need to provide users with access to multimedia information quickly and interactively through the integration of technologies.

— The need to transfer a large volume of data and/or files from one system to another.

The following will discuss briefly the technologies available for mass storage and the types of storage media as well as the drives available for using these media.

Various technologies available for mass storage Traditionally libraries have used conventional media like film, microfilm and microfiche to store information materials, but they are bulky and rather expensive.

With the advent of computer and optical technologies, mass storage has shifted mostly to electronic media. There are several different technologies available for mass storage on magnetic tapes, high-density floppy disks, portable hard disks with a capacity of over 2 GB, and optical disks. But it is optical media that are the primary ones for mass storage.

Because of this, the following section will explore further the different types of optical media. Storage media: optical disks, CD-ROM, etc. The various types of optical media offer different storage densities, media formats, transfer rates, capabilities and compatibility among commercial vendors' products.

In the last decade alone, a flood of new media and applications—CD-ROM, laser videodisks, write-once and read-many devices, erasable disks, to name just a few—have been introduced, promoted and utilized. There is a wide range of optical alternatives available to provide the highest application flexibility to end-users. Optical media can be grouped into three major categories:

— Read-only media.

— Write-once and read-many.

— Erasable.

Under each of these major categories, a multitude of optical storage media can be found. For more detailed information on each of these optical media. All of them are essential for multimedia application developments.

Drive and interface

Each different kind of optical media requires an appropriate drive to be connected to a microcomputer system. Multimedia CD-ROMs have become popular products in recent years. Earlier, interactive videodisks were the popular means of presenting multimedia applications. Even today, some applications still choose videodisks as end products if quantities of still and moving images are large. For example, one side of a videodisk can store 58,000 still images and thirty minutes of video in dual sound tracks. These are huge in comparison to what can be stored digitally on a multimedia CD-ROM even with high-ratio compression. For the latter, we are talking about a few hundred digital images and less than twenty minutes of digital video in small windows. Thus, videodisk disk applications are still substantial. The major manufacturers of videodisk players are Philips, Pioneer and Sony. Each has produced several different models—industrial or general models with different playing speeds, and some with the capability of playing both NTSC (National Television System Committee) and PAL (Phase Alternation Line) disks.

CD-ROM drives

The CD-ROM drive is currently the most popular device; it can be used to play regular CD-ROMs (mostly text-based) and Photo-CDs as well as multimedia CD-ROMs. Speed is one of the most significant considerations when acquiring such a drive. In order to run a multimedia CD-ROM, the minimum requirement is a double-speed (2X) drive. However, 4-speed and even 6-speed are available in the marketplace. The 4-speed drive is very affordable and can be purchased for less then US$200 per unit in the United States.

CD recorders

WORM and erasable drives are essential for mass storage, publishing and back-up of multimedia development materials. Earlier WORM drives played discs generally holding 100 MB to 200 MB of data. The latest WORM CD medium is CD-R (CD-Recordable) which can store 600 MB of data and requires a CD recorder with appropriate software to record information on the disc according to the appropriate CD standard. For example, JVC's Personal RomMaker, Kodak's PCD Writer and Philips' CDD 522 Compact Disc Recorder are only a few samples of such CD recording devices with hardware and software solutions that allow users to premaster and master their own CD-ROMs in-house on the desktop for both PC and Mac platforms. Optical Media's TOPiX is a CD publishing system used to record information on CD. Once the information is recorded, the disc will be used in the same manner as any other CD-ROM by using a regular CD-ROM drive. It goes without saying that for multimedia application development, such CD recording devices are most useful!

Erasable drives

For multimedia work, no matter how big the size of the hard drive, one will quickly run out of storage space. Thus every multimedia product developer has some kind of device that can expand the hard drive's capacity substantially. Such devices are also used to back up the materials on the hard drive. An erasable medium is very attractive for this purpose as it can be modified and/or re-used. However, erasable optical disk technology is still not very stable, and both the medium and the drive are quite expensive. An erasable drive can cost over US$2,000. Thus, one of the more popular products has been the SyQuest drive; each SyQuest cartridge can store from 44 MB to about 200 MB of data/information. Two of the hottest products in this line now are Iomega's Zip and Zap drives, which are both easy to use and affordable. The Zip drive, which runs with its Zip disk (100 MB per disk) costs only a meagre $199 per drive and the disk is less than $20, depending on the quantity purchased (over ten will cost only $14.99 per disk). The Zap drive, with a disk capacity as big as 1 GB, costs only around $599. Because of this incredible offer, many personal computer manufacturers have decided to include a Zip drive as part of the regular system configuration.

Multimedia operating and file system Multimedia hardware and peripherals. To enter the interactive multimedia world, a minimum equipment configuration should be more than the bare minimum described earlier. It should consist of the following components:

— A computer system with a minimum of 4 MB of RAM.

— A 350 MB hard disk drive.

— A 14.4 kbps modem (fax modem would be preferable).

— A double-speed CD-ROM drive.

— A portable videotape recorder.

A fixed videotape recorder capable of being connected to a computer output either directly or through an appropriate AV card inserted into one of the bus slots in the computer. A television monitor for use during taping and playback.

— A scanner.

Additional hardware in the form of an LCD display panel or LCD projection system is highly recommended.

The minimum software configuration for using multimedia products is rather low, since most products have plug-and-play capabilities with very few requirements other than the installation processes. However, the following are varying levels of software requirements for producing simple multimedia applications:

— A basic editing software package, such as those available from Adobe, Avid, Radius and others.

— An intermediate-level software system that would include all of the above plus a freestanding audio editing software package, a two-dimensional modelling or rendering software package and a graphic/titling package such as Adobe Photoshop.

— An advanced-level software system that would include all the above plus an advanced-level three-dimensional modelling or rendering software package, and an authorware package for output to hard, floppy disk or to read/write compact disc.

The equipment cost varies greatly from one model to another, and from one configuration to another. Thus it is best to check with the vendors for current price information. However, it is safe to estimate that a PC

Pentium multimedia system can be acquired from US$1,500 to $4,000, and a Macintosh Power Mac from US$2,000 to $5,500, depending on the system model, RAM size, hard disk size, and connected peripherals. Whenever possible, efforts should be made to acquire a system with as large a RAM and hard disk storage capacity as possible. The cost of software also varies greatly, ranging from less than $100 to over $1,000. However, powerful software like Adobe Photoshop costs about $600 and Macromedia's Director about $900.

The abundant multimedia tools are to be used for creating multimedia applications. Yet how one goes about developing multimedia depends on the nature of the application and how it will be viewed and used. Although there is no multimedia development formula, the process does follow a series of basic steps. These steps include:

— Concept.

— Content and interface.

— Product.

It is impossible in a short paper like this to cover every aspect of the process, but each major step, and the subsets within each step.

Planning and design is always the most important component of any development, regardless of whether it is technology-related or not. Usually at least half to two-thirds of project effort is devoted to this phase. In other words, the better a project is planned and designed, the more likely it is that it will be successful, effective, efficient and useful. For a multimedia application, after the idea is conceived and a conceptual framework developed, the planning process will have to go into the more minute details of plans and design, so that these will lead to the successful implementation of the application development. Many questions will have to be addressed:

— What are the goals and objectives of the application?

— Who is it intended for?

— What is it going to deliver which is either not available or not sufficiently available now?

— What is the delivery platform?

— What multimedia elements will the application include?

— What are the existing information sources and which and how will these be used for the application?

— Where can help and/or contributions be found?

— What is the budget for the application, and how will it be budgeted?

— What are the environmental limitations?

— What existing multimedia tools - both hardware and software - are required?

— Who is going to do what?

— How will it be published?

— What is the target completion date?

Once these questions have been addressed, the multimedia developer can deal with all the problems and issues surfacing during both the pre-production and production periods. It is important to stress the importance of project design. This includes both the application design and interface design. Remember that an application can deal with 'gold-mine' source materials which are rich, relevant and essential, but if the presentation is not well thought out and the interactive feature of multimedia technology is not fully utilized, then the richness of the available knowledge base will not be fully exploited. On the other hand, even if the presentation of the multimedia application is well designed conceptually, it can still fail if the interface design is either poor or uninviting/confusing to the user. Few would be willing or able to visit the 'gold-mine'.

Design criteria for effective integration of different media In designing multimedia applications, it is essential to realize that the process of linking multimedia information in a hyperweb environment can be both confusing and disorienting. The following multimedia functionalities under three categories - essential, expected and desirable:

Essential	*Expected*	*Desirable*
Integration	Diversity	Programmability
Freedom	Extensibility	Orientability
Flexibility	Sociality	Guidability
Usability	Spatiality	Recreatability
Attributability	Communicability	

One needs to remember that beyond the many demanding technical elements that allow multimedia to come together, there is a sense of transcendentalness that occurs during the production process. While combining massive amounts of information, one commonly observes coincidences and encounters baffling developments. Great care must be taken to separate the intelligent realities from the illusions. Integrating the complex threads of interactive electronic communication requires an emphasis on the relationship between the designer/producers and their reader/listener/user/viewer. New access paths to source material and new procedures for protection and licensing must be developed. Industry standards must emerge to facilitate diversity and universal connectivity.

Preparation of Multimedia Documents

After the planning, one has to determine what kind of information is to be included and published, and then prepare and process this information. Information sources can include all formats - textual, still images and motion videos, sounds and animation. This step involves information-gathering and preparation, and electronic management. The former determines the format to be chosen for inclusion, and the latter considers how to turn all the desired information to electronic forms and also how to manage them.

Data preparation and processing

Text: The existing text information can be available in both printed and electronic forms. For the printed information, all three popular ways of conversion to an electronic format - keyboarding, imaging (scanning), and optical character recognition - will be used. For the electronic files, once the delivery platform is decided, electronic text files will have to be converted for the chosen platform.

Images: Hard-copy images will have to be scanned and stored in acceptable format for multimedia applications. The most popular format is JPEG (Joint

Photographic Experts Group), but PICT (a Macintosh graphics file format, closely related to PCT and commonly supported in Macintosh format) and TIFF (Tag Image FileFormats) are also popular with multimedia application software. When multimedia is moving closely with Internet and World Wide Web applications, GIF and JPEG with a very high rate of compression are preferred. Scanned images often need to be processed and enhanced by the use of software like Adobe Photoshop.

Video: Using the video-capturing software via a video-capturing board, one can convert video sources from television, video recorder and video camera to digital video and save them in popular formats such as QuickTime movies (in both platforms), or AVI (Audio-Video Interleaved) for PC applications. The standard for digital video is MPEG (Moving Pictures Experts Group). Again, liked the scanned images, captured digital videos will have to be edited by the use of software tools like Macro-media's Director, Adobe's Premier or Avid's VideoShop.

Sound: Through the use of sound recording software and a sound recorder, sound sources from tapes, cassettes and video can be converted to digital sound files, which can also be manipulated and enhanced by means of existing tools, some of them described earlier in this paper. Data compression for digitized data, sound and fixed and moving images Non-text files consume a large amount of storage space (for example, one colour image at screen resolution can easily take up about 1 MB of disk space or more); thus the issue of size becomes very significant, and hence compression and decompression. Compression is a widely employed technique to reduce the size of large files without appreciably changing the way a viewer sees the images or digital videos or hears the sounds. Once compressed, the file must be decompressed before it can be used. Compression and decompression can be accomplished by software alone or through the use of a combination of software and hardware. Take image as an example: compression software analyses an image and finds ways to store the same amount of information using less storage space. Compression hardware usually consists of a ROM chip with built-in compression routines for faster operation, or a co-processor chip that shares the computing load with the computer's main processor. There are different levels of software compression:

— *Lossless compression:* no information lost through the compression process. In this way, the file size is generally not reduced much.

— *Lossy compression:* through the compression, some information is lost. This will reduce the file size more dramatically than the lossless one.

The most common method for compressing image is called JPEG, which is a standard way of reducing image file size that discards information which could not be detected easily by the human eye. In compressing the digital video, the standard is MPEG. MPEG is an industry standard for moving images that uses interframe compression (or frame differencing) as well as compression within frames. There are different MPEG standards, such as MPEG I, which optimizes for data rates in the 1 to 1.5 MB/sec range (the common transfer rate of CD-ROM drives and T-1 communications links), and MPEG II, which optimizes for data rates above the 5 MB/sec rate (specifically for broadcast video applications).

There are many compelling reasons for using multimedia for education, training, information delivery, business, entertainment, etc. First of all, the power of pictures is enormous. Only recently, with the advent of multimedia technologies, have we been able to tap the undeniable power of visual images and other non-textual information sources. But equally appealing for multimedia technology is the power of interactivity - a concept extended from hypertext as discussed in the introductory section. Through the ages, information has been presented and absorbed in a linear fashion. Interactive multimedia brings the incredible freedom to explore a subject area with fast links to related topics.

Storage and use of digital data and documents

Mass storage and storage media were discussed above. Currently, most digital data have been stored on optical media such as CD-ROMs, CD-Rs, and Photo-CDs, and most interactive multimedia products are produced and distributed as multimedia CD-ROMs, or interactive laser disks. The portability of these products, specifically those on CD-ROMs,is great.

When multimedia applications are stored or published on an optical medium such as CD-ROM, they can be distributed easily for intra-organization-aluse. For a few copies, in-house CD-R technology can be used to produce the CD-ROMs. When published formally, whether commercially or not, the CD-ROMs or laser disks will be mastered by companies like 3M, DMI, Philips, etc. The cost of production generally is around US$1,000 to $1,500, with an additional cost for each unit ranging from $1.50 to over $10 depending on the quantity of the order.

Commercially produced CD-ROMs are generally published and distributed much like books, and they will be properly packaged with an attractive graphically designed cover, and publicized for sale either directly from the publisher or via distributors, or both. Currently over 10,000 multimedia products have been published.

Use and reuse of stored documents. When information source materials are in digital form and stored electronically on a digital medium, they can be used and reused for any suitable purpose. They can be retrieved easily to answer an information inquiry, used to create multimedia applications, or used for resource-sharing in either a network environment or for electronic publishing on the Internet or the World Wide Web. The important thing is being digital!

We are very much aware of the need to back up electronic data with additional copies of floppy disks, backup tapes, Zip or Zap disks, or CD-Rs. It is important to add that optical media, specifically something like CD-ROM, tend to give an impression that they are the ultimate conservation medium with no possibility of data loss. Actually this is not the case.

The lifetime of optical media such as CD-ROM, suggesting thirty years or more. However, it is difficult to verify the accuracy of these predictions at this time. All electronic media have the possibility of wearing out, and thus it is important to make duplicate copies in order to avoid data loss due to wear and tear. Optical media such as CD-ROMs and laser disks should be used carefully to prevent possible scratches on the surface. Non-optical electronic media, such as magnetic tape and floppy disks, should be stored under proper temperature and humidity control.

As for the storage of the source materials, it is important to continue finding the best ways to preserve and conserve them regardless of whether they are electronic or not. Most images and videos originally came from film or microfilm sources. These should be kept using the best conservation methods, since electronic image-capturing - still or moving -cannot currently produce images of as high a resolution as those on films and microfilms. Thus, as tech-nologiesadvance, there will be need still to reuse the source materials in order to produce new images of higher resolution.

Emerging Technologies and Fure Trends

As the use of multimedia will continue to expand, it is fair to expect that more tools in every category outlined earlier will be introduced with more functionalities and at lower cost. Thus, creating multimedia applications will be easier as time goes on.

With the explosive development and use of the Internet and the World Wide Web, and the exponential growth in use of Web browsers like Netscape, we are witnessing the exciting marriage of multimedia and the Internet/World Wide Web in a way never possible before.

Instead of Web publishing with mainly still images, graphics and text, now virtual reality and Web publishing with avitars are being introduced by all major companies like Netscape and Microsoft. The forthcoming versions of Web browsers, like the 3.0 version of Netscape, are filled with all kinds of features and capabilities to present digital videos, sound, animations, etc.

In addition to the increasing capability to include all types of multimedia publishing on the Web, emerging technologies will enable exciting live multimedia Internet publishing as well as real-time fast delivery of multimedia broadcasting onto the desktop.

A good example of live multimedia Internet publishing is the '24 Hours in Cyberspace' event on 8 February 1996. On that day, Rick Smolan, producer of award-winning multimedia products such as From Alice to Ocean and Passage to Vietnam, pulled off the most ambitious Internet event ever undertaken by deploying hundreds of speed global network so that texts, images and even voices can be transmitted from one part of the world to another.

At the same time, however, nationalism becomes a stronger theme: building national collections, serving as an information source for national government, and collecting national history or culture are of concern now more than ever.

The use of multimedia and Knowledge Navigator permit the delivery of this information, as well as information from other countries, to citizens' homes, schools and offices. In this kind of environment, printed information sources, such as books, journals and archival materials, meet a highly competitive technology.

Digital information sources become essential. The enormous possibilities for combining multimedia and the Internet/World Wide Web together have also been demonstrated. At the click of an icon, to jump to any national library or other major library in a given country instantly. Access can also be gained to information on the award-winning multimedia product, The First Emperor of China.

As long as the resources are in digital format - regardless of whether they are still images, video or sound - and are on a Web server, one can obtain this information almost instantly from anywhere in the world. A graphic directory of over thirty national library homepages around the world can be found in Chen. This is an exciting time!

Telecommunication Technologies

Telecommunication technologies have been changing the nature of personal and business transactions since the commercialization of the telegraph in the 1840s. The synergy between information service providers and telecommunication carriers was recognized in the United States as early as 1867, when an exclusive contract between Associated Press and Western Union was signed. The impact of telecommunication control on information dissemination has been researched by many authors since then. But telecommunication is more than a means of information dissemination; it also provides information users with a means of searching out and interacting with information. With the emergence of digital computers, information became represented more frequently in digital format, so that it became possible to search databases and transfer information from remote locations. This trend began with large corporations and their centralized databases and has since permeated many aspects of life in industrialized countries, especially with the emergence of the World Wide Web on the Internet.

Since the 1980s the use of computer-based information retrieval systems has become popular with many libraries and information service providers. In many public libraries, computer-based catalogues have replaced their traditional card counterparts, offering capabilities such as simultaneous access by multiple users, keyword searching and remote access. With the emergence of the CD-ROM, much original information has become accessible over computer networks. This paper addresses many of the key questions surrounding the basic technology and its application to the information industry.

This section defines and describes the requirements for the most common forms of services in use by information service providers. Many of these require telecommunication technologies, although analogous services are often available without this technological infrastructure. In subsequent sections, the commonly used implementations and infrastructure requirements will be described.

Remote access is a user's ability to make use of an information provider's services at a distance. This is desirable because it enables information service providers to economize their operations (through appropriate centralization) without eliminating access for distant users. Thus, a large population of users can be served without extensive need to travel.

Traditionally, remote access has involved the use of postal or telephone inquiries. This method has a number of both advantages and disadvantages over electronic information technology solutions. These can be summarized under three main headings: cost, training and speed. Traditional remote-access technology is more labour-intensive but less capital-intensive; electronic technologies are more capital-intensive and require skilled 'backroom' personnel, but fewer information specialists. Traditional remote-access technology requires virtually no user training but considerable information-specialist training; electronic remote access requires user training as well as computer professionals. Finally, traditional remote access is very slow by comparison to electronic access.

Electronic remote access generally requires users' data terminals to connect to an information service provider's serving computer. This connection may be handled via a modem and telephone lines or a public or private packet data network. When connected to the service provider's computer, users are able to interact with the system as though they were local to the service provider's computer. In the Internet, the Telnet service is an example of this service type; in Open Systems Interconnection (OSI) systems, this service would be the Virtual Terminal (VT) service. Electronic remote access also implies a reliable, high-quality telecommunication infrastructure.

Remote access implies that the information being sought remains at the server when the session is over. If any information is retained by the user, such as notes or printouts, it is generally a small fraction of the information and is not kept in digital form. If the user wishes to acquire pieces of information of a larger size, then a file transfer operation is usually preferred. Traditionally, this might involve the acquisition, either in person or via the postal system, of books, journals, articles, etc. This analogy is not perfect because electronic file transfer allows pieces of information to be transferred that may not exist in print or other traditional media.

While file transfers can be accomplished using remote-access services (if the user's device has sufficient capabilities), this operation is limited and not efficient. Using file transfer mechanisms instead enables the efficient transfer of both text and non-text characters without the insertion of special characters. Furthermore, most file transfer protocols have additional error-checking functionality built into them. Thus, information transfers can take place completely and efficiently. Commonly used file transfer protocols are ftp for the Internet, and File Transfer, Access and Management (FTAM) for OSI-based information systems. Electronic messaging

The most common form of this technology is electronic mail, although it need not be limited to this. The objective in electronic messaging technologies is to allow the efficient transfer of messages of all kinds between the users of a network (humans as well as machines). Recent research has taken a broader view of this question and considers the use of still, animated and video images, as well as audio, graphics and text, to pass messages. In this broader context, then, 'voice mail' is also a form of electronic messaging.

Numerous standards exist for electronic mail. By far the most widely implemented standard is Internet mail. Designed to support the transfer of text files only, this standard has been modified to support non-text information, such as images and binary files, through the Multimedia Internet Mail Extensions (MIME) system.

As with most Internet standards, these represent relatively limited, although highly functional, solutions to specific problems. In response to the more comprehensive needs of the user community, the International

Telecommunications Union (ITU) developed the X.400 series of standards. These standards represent a systematic and comprehensive approach to meeting the needs of electronic mail users. The implementation is much more complex, hence costly, than Internet mail; as a result, it has yet to be adopted as widely.

Database searching is an application that is increasingly network-based. The databases that are searched were organized historically as a single database on a single machine. This is gradually changing with the introduction of distributed databases, in which the database is logically a single database but is physically distributed over several computers. Many of the CD-ROM-based databases seem to exhibit this characteristic, although they are frequently a collection of independent databases that must be queried separately.

Traditionally, database searches have been performed by attaching to the computer that houses the database a remote-access protocol (such as Telnet) and executing queries on the database. In recent years, searches based on the American National Standards Institution/National Information Standards Organization (ANSI/NISO) standard Z39.50 and Z39.59 have begun eliminating the need for users to connect directly with, and therefore have accounts on, remote database machines. These standards allow for the delivery of query results to an end-user using a standardized remote-access protocol. This mode of database searching is more efficient and flexible for both the network and the database machines, so it can be expected to be implemented more widely in the future.

On the World Wide Web, search engines (such as Lycos and Yahoo) have emerged to facilitate information searching in this decentralized environment. These systems create an index of Web pages that can be searched. The results of these searches are brief descriptions of a page and the links to those pages. These are different from traditional database-searching systems in that the search engines must actively compile and update information, since the World Wide Web is perhaps the ultimate example of a distributed and decentralized database in which no attempt at consistency is made.

Electronic Data Interchange (EDI) is the direct computer-to-computer exchange of information. While this is a very general definition, EDI is really focused on the exchange of information normally provided in business documents such as bills of lading, purchase orders and invoices. With the emergence of EDI standards, such as EDIFACT and ANSI X.12,EDI has gained significant popularity. When both partners in a transaction use compatible EDI systems, the benefits of using this approach over traditional mechanisms include cost savings, speed, error reduction and security. EDI standards define specific transaction sets that in turn define the way in which information is to be communicated; a transaction set is the equivalent of a form in a paper-based communication system. A transaction set must have certain content and format specifications to ensure that both parties can interpret the information correctly. Just as a form has 'boxes' for information, a transaction set has segments that contain defined data elements.

computer systems that are interconnected by telecommunication technology. This section will present an overview of the telecommunication technologies that are relevant to the user needs defined above.

Physical infrastructure

In broad terms, the physical infrastructure consists of three components: cables, switching systems and signalling systems. Cables are used to interconnect devices, switches are used to route calls through the network (over cables), and signalling systems allow network devices (such as telephones and switches) to exchange information. This section will summarize each of these components.

Cables

The physical infrastructure consists of a combination of cables and their associated outside plant. The primary types of cables in use are twisted pair, optical fibre and coaxial. Twisted-pair cables consist of two insulated wires twisted together; these types of cable are most often used to connect the subscriber's equipment with the telephone network. Optical fibre is used most often for high-capacity transmission within the network, that is, to connect large subscribers. Finally, coaxial cables are used both within the telephone network and for high-bandwidth transmission to subscribers' premises, as in cable television applications. The former use is being replaced by fibre optics, while the latter use is fairly well developed and embedded.

Wireless infrastructures have been important since the 1940s, but the locus of their use has changed. Early non-broadcast uses of wireless were focused on interconnecting telephone company facilities using point-to-point microwave systems or satellite-based systems. The emergence of fibre optics as a technically and economically viable technology in the 1980s has stimulated the replacement of existing wireless facilities of this kind and limited the new installations to situations where cable is not feasible. Today, the use of wireless is focused more on connecting 'nomadic' or 'untethered' subscribers. Cellular, General System for Mobile (GSM) and Personal Communications System (PCS) systems are examples of this use.

Switching

While many other elements do exist, the other key element of the infrastructure is switches. Switches serve to interconnect subscribers with each other, either directly (if they are local) or via other switches and interoffice transmission facilities (if they are not local). In order to function properly, the devices on the network must pass certain information to each other, such as 'off-hook' and 'on-hook' (which corresponds to 'busy' and 'idle') and the dialled number. The mechanism by which this information is passed is the signalling system.

Switching technology has undergone a radical evolution since the early days of telephony. The simplest (and also the earliest) switches consisted of a panel of electrical jacks, one for each subscriber and trunk (as an inter office transmission channel is called). A human operator connected subscribers with each other (or to trunks) using patch cords with plugs on both ends. In the

United States, these manual systems were gradually replaced with electromechanical switches during the early part of the twentieth century. In the 1960s, these electromechanical switches began to be replaced by digital electronic switches. In other countries, this investment/ replacement cycle may not be consistent with the experience of the United States.

Signalling technology also has changed. The earliest signalling consisted of sharply rapping the transmitter to get the attention of the operator or called party. This was soon replaced by a combination of magneto and bell. The destination number was originally spoken into the telephone by the caller to the operator, who would complete the call. As automated switches and digit dialling came into service, these signalling functions were replaced by in-band techniques. As the network grew in size, and as electronic switches were introduced, it became possible to introduce out-of-band signalling systems, such as Signalling System 7, that allow faster call setup and the implementation of new services.

Out-of-band signalling systems, like Signalling System 7, are implemented by creating a packet-switched data communications network, and treating the voice switches and service providers as users of the network. The messages and protocols are standardized and optimized for the rapid exchange of short messages between these devices. Many ISDN (Integrated Services Digital Network) systems require a Signalling System 7 infrastructure.

speech is converted to electrical energy by a microphone. Microphones create an electrical signal that is modulated in proportion to the strength and characteristics of the speech energy. Commercially available microphones always generate an electrical signal that is continuous in time; such a signal is called an analogue signal. Voice telecommunications were transmitted in analogue format throughout the telephone network until the 1960s.

As an electrical signal is transmitted over distance, it is subject to certain deleterious effects, most notably noise and distortion. Noise consists of all unwanted electrical signals that are added to the signal in the transmission channel. Distortion is generally due to imperfections in the design of transmission equipment. Neither noise nor distortion can be avoided. Many types of noise are additive; that is, they are added to the signal in the transmission channel. As the distance increases, more noise and distortion is added, so that, as a rule, the signal deteriorates as distance increases. In an analogue system, the noise and distortion cannot be removed from the signal at the receiver because of the continuous nature of both the signal, noise and distortion.

In the 1940s researchers at Bell Laboratories developed methods by which an analogue signal could be sampled in such a way that the samples could be used to reconstruct an accurate facsimile of the original signal. When a signal is sampled in this way, it becomes possible to represent these samples by a number that is proportional to the strength of the analogue electrical signal at the time it was sampled. Since this number can be represented in any number system, the engineers chose the binary number system. In the binary system, the number takes the form of multiple digits (eight, in the case of telephony) comprising only ones and zeros.

The primary advantage of representing a signal and transmitting it in this way is that the essential information contained in the signal is in discrete levels rather than in continuous levels. Thus, when the signal with the added noise and distortion arrives at the receiver, the receiver can remove much of the noise because it can reconstruct the signal that was transmitted based on the discrete levels (if the system was properly engineered). It is possible to engineer a digital transmission system with very low noise levels. Since binary numbers are in the format that is natural for computational devices, it is also possible to engineer a reliable transmission system through long and noisy channels using sophisticated signal processing and error detection and correction techniques. The spacecraft that send pictures to Earth from distant planets provide an example of such a demanding environment.

Data and voice communications

When speech is rendered as a digital signal, the distinction between voice signals and data signals begins to become arbitrary, since neither the switches nor the network equipment can distinguish between them. None the less, the services that are constructed on the network infrastructure to support voice applications and data applications are different. These different applications place different demands on the network infrastructure. Voice communications, whether analogue or digital, historically have been implemented by dedicating a portion of the network capacity to a call for the duration of that call.

No other call can use the bandwidth dedicated to that call. For data applications, this arrangement was wasteful, since the line was idle for a large fraction of the time. Communications between computers are frequently 'bursty', that is, communication between devices occurs infrequently but when it does the devices need a fast connection for modest quantities of data. As a result, engineers developed mechanisms for sharing a line's bandwidth among several simultaneous but different calls so that the line would be utilized more efficiently.

The most widely adopted technique for this uses a set of technologies referred to collectively as packet switching. In packet switching, several data streams are bundled and transmitted together by sending a small portion of each data stream at a time in the form of a 'packet'. Each packet contains the address of the destination computer as well as other necessary control information, so that the packet switches (special purpose computers in the data communications network) have the information to handle each packet. The packet switches collect traffic from many computers and determine how to direct each packet so that it reaches its destination (a function called routing).

While packet-switched networks clearly provided a more economical solution for data communications applications, packets can arrive with a variable delay because all facilities in the network are shared by all packets in the network. Although this is not troublesome for most data applications, it can pose difficulties when traffic, such as voice traffic, is routed through packet networks. New network technologies, such as those based on the Asynchronous Transfer Mode (ATM), are seeking to solve these difficulties so that a single network infrastructure can be constructed for all major telecommunications applications.

Integrated services digital network (ISDN) ISDN is an approach to extend the digitization of the telephone network to the user's telephone. It is defined by a set of ITU standards that were developed in large part during the 1980s. Today, these original services are known as Narrowband ISDN, or N-ISDN. In recent years, the ISDN concept has been extended to highspeed services under the auspices of Broadband ISDN (or B-ISDN). This section will focus on N-ISDN, since those services today are defined and supported by commercially available equipment and services.

ISDN goes beyond a simple definition of a digital signalling and transmission standard for the local loop (which connects the user's telephone with the telephone switch). It defines an architecture for the delivery of a comprehensive set of integrated services over an end-to-end digital architecture. This architecture includes the standards for the necessary hardware, communications protocols and software functionality.

From a user's point of view, the most common N-ISDN services that can be purchased are the Basic Rate Interface (BRI) and Primary Rate Interface (PRI) services. Residential subscribers are most likely to purchase the BRI service, since it consists of the digital equivalent of two voice lines and a data line. In digital terms, each of the two voice lines is a channel with a bit rate of 64,000 bits per second (a 64 kbps channel, in telecommunications jargon). In ISDN terminology, channels that carry information at 64 kbps are called 'bearer' channels (or B-channels). The BRI signalling channel (data or D-channel) has a 16 kbps bit rate. The D-channel is used to provide services to the subscriber, including basic services such as call setup. Because of its configuration, BRI ISDN is often referred to as a '2B + D' configuration because it consists of two B-channels and a D-channel.

For large users, such as businesses, a collection of BRI channels may not be ideal as they would lack flexibility. Such organizations would normally opt to purchase a Primary Rate Interface or PRI service. Unlike BRI, users under PRI can choose several channel configurations. Thus, PRI users (in the United States) might choose a 23 B + D service, a H0 + 17B + D service, or others. Users must negotiate the specifics of the interface with their service provider. Much more could be said about ISDN in terms of its functionality and its role in organizations. In brief, ISDN provides users with the capability of true end-to-end digitial connectivity with other users and service providers. Furthermore, ISDN provides much higher data rates than can be achieved using modems, with the possibility of having value-enhancing services integrated with the transport.

ISDN's bearer and highspeed channels provide basic transport for a user's voice and data. Functionally, this is similar to the traditional analogue channel provided by telecommunication service providers (although the equipment varies). When computers are communicating, new demands are placed on both the network and on the end-user devices—demands that do not exist in voice communications.

As computer networks evolved, many more problems had to be addressed in addition to that of 'bursty' traffic. These include error control, synchronization, security and information representation. It also became apparent that standards were important in computer networks. Two major groups of standards have emerged for computer networks - the standards consistent with the OSI Reference Model and developed by the ITU and the International Standards Organization (ISO), and the standards that emerged out of the ARPANET project in the United States, which are referred to as the Internet Standards.

Open systems interconnection (OSI)

The OSI Reference Model and its associated standards (generally referred to as OSI standards) emerged in the late 1970s. The origins of this movement are complex, but include user frustration with incompatibility between large system vendors and concern among the smaller of the large system vendors about the dominance of one company, IBM.

The OSI Reference Model is a systematic approach to the generic data communications problem. It organizes communication in seven layers, each of which is assigned specific functionality. The bottom three layers (1-3) are network-related layers in that they explicitly involve network components. The upper layers (4-7) are end-to-end, and do not involve network components. Specifically, the data communications function is organized as follows:

Physical layer (1): Standards that relate to the physical and electrical interconnection of computing or networking devices, and standards related to the encoding and physical transmission of bits over a communications medium.

Link layer (2): Standards that relate to the transmission of information on a single medium. This includes error control, framing, synchronization and local addressing.

Network layer (3): Standards related to the transmission of information across several links and nodes. This includes global addressing and routing.

Transport layer (4): Standards related to the transport of information from end to end over a network. This may include multiplexing of a connection between several user processes and end-to-end error control.

Session layer (5): Standards that define naming and control for multiple connections associated with a single user process.

Presentation layer (6): Standards that are concerned with the representation of information.

Application layer (7): Standards that define protocols to support higher-level user functions.

Internationally, one of the most important data communications standards is the X.25 developed by the ITU. The X.25 standard defines the interface between a user's equipment (Data Terminal Equipment, or DTE) and the network (Data Communications Equipment, or DCE) at the network, link and physical layers of the OSI Reference Model. The X.25 standard is formally limited to speeds of 64 kbps and lower, although higher-speed implementations can sometimes be found. X.25 uses the High speed Data Link Control (HDLC) protocol at the link layer and the X.21 physical layer connection.

Since the X.25 Packet Layer Protocol (PLP) operates at Layer 3 of the OSI Reference Model, it must use globally unique addresses: X.25 uses the X.121 global addressing scheme developed by the ITU. Since X.25 only defines the interface between DTE and DCE, it does not define the manner in which data are handled within a packet network. In fact, different commercial networks use various protocols and network control techniques internally. X.25 does not make specific statements about the operation of a packet network; it merely addresses the interfaces to the network.

X.25 is a connection-oriented network protocol because the protocol requires that a virtual circuit be established in the network before information can be transferred. A virtual circuit is a route through the network that all packets between the users will follow. It is a virtual circuit because it is not dedicated to the two parties, as it would be in a telephone connection; it merely behaves as though it were, even though the physical bandwidth is shared among many users.

X.25 assumes a relatively unreliable network infrastructure from the point of view of bit errors. Thus, error checking and correcting is done on each link as it passes through the network. This process turns out to be very time-consuming, limiting the effective throughput of X.25 networks. As networks have improved over the last twenty-five years with the introduction of optical fibre and digital transmission, this performance penalty has become increasingly apparent, resulting in technologies such as frame relay, which forgo link-by-link error checking in favour of end-to-end error checking.

X.400 and X.500 standards

ITU's X.400 series of standards provides for a comprehensive approach to electronic mail services. It gives service providers a broad range of services that can be offered to their customers. This richness comes at the expense of ease of implementation and product cost, factors that have delayed the implementation and adoption of products based on the X.400 series of standards. X.400 is a series of standards because it consists of a number of distinct, albeit interrelated, elements. These elements include User Agents (UAs), Message Transfer Agents (MTAs) and several service elements, as well as the protocols by which these elements communicate with one another. The message body can contain information in text, facsimile, video, image, telex, videotex and other formats. The X.500 series of standards is designed to support the development of directory services. A directory service is a system-level capability that allows users to find the 'symbolic name' (or address) of a user or a service. Broadly speaking, a directory service supports not only the binding of a symbolic name with an entity (such as a user or a resource), but also allows for the management of that information in a systematic and structured way.

The developers of the Transmission Control Protocol/Internet Protocol (TCP/IP) suite originally solved this problem in a decentralized way by using the Domain Name System (DNS). X.500 considered the directory problem from a global and commercial perspective, and in the light of experience with X.25. Thus, they developed a hierarchical system that allows a system of locally maintained Directory Service Agents (DSAs) to be tied together into a logical tree structure. A DSA communicates with as many other DSAs as necessary, using the standard protocols defined by X.500, to resolve requests from an attached Directory User Agent (DUA).

TCP/IP protocols

The TCP/IP protocols, referred to above, are an

important suite of protocols for data communications, developed under the auspices of the United States Department of Defense. These protocols have gained considerable commercial popularity and are the foundation of the Internet. Unlike the ITU and ISO standards, the TCP/IP-based protocols evolved through a collegial, informal process that emphasized working implementations. As a result, these protocols are often focused on a 'simple' solution to a specific problem without considering (and sometimes explicitly ignoring) broader functionality and systematic design. Despite these shortcomings, these protocols always produce working prototypes that may be (and often are) adapted for use in commercial products.

The TCP/IP protocol suite consists of a set of lower-layer protocols (often Local Area Network standards such as Ethernet and Token Ring), a net-work-layer protocol (Internet Protocol, or IP), a transport-layer protocol (such as Transmission Control Protocol, or TCP), and application protocols (for example, Simple Mail Transfer Protocol, smtp; File Transfer Protocol, ftp; and a virtual terminal protocol, Telnet). This approach completely omits the session and presentation layers. Unlike the X.25 packet-layer protocol (which is connection-oriented), IP is connectionless.

In a connectionless protocol, no virtual circuit is established at the outset; instead, each packet contains the source and destination addresses of the end-users, and each packet is routed through the network independently. As a result, packets may take different paths through the network and arrive out of order. The network provides no guarantees to the end-users, leaving error control to them. IP provides global addressing (but not via X.121). The number of available IP addresses has become limited owing to the structure of IP addressing and the explosive growth of the Internet.

A new version of IP (IP version 6) is due to be released in the near future to tackle that problem. The most commonly used transport layer, TCP, is connection-oriented and provides end-to-end error control as well as flow control. Given the military environment that was assumed when TCP and IP were developed, the combinations of protocols make sense. IP is very resistant to node and line failures, since the connectionless packets automatically find an available path to the destination. TCP ensures that messages arrive error-free at the destination in a way that does not excessively congest the network.

The TCP/IP set of protocols has been a favourite of many academic researchers because it is extraordinarily flexible and amenable to experimentation. As a result, new concepts and services, such as the gopher information retrieval protocol and the World Wide Web concept (with its associated protocols and standards) are able to emerge quickly and easily.

Governments and international organizations have been intimately involved in telecommunication from its inception. The United States Government financed Samuel F. B. Morse's experimental telegraph line between Baltimore (Maryland) and Washington, D.C., in 1837. In most countries the government soon entered the business by building networks and providing telegraph (and later telephone) services. As telegraph (and later telephone) systems expanded in Europe, it soon became necessary to interconnect separate national systems.

This interconnection imperative motivated the development of technical standards as well as guidelines for negotiating the terms and conditions of interconnection. Out of this need, the predecessor of the ITU was born. It did not take long for this need for interconnection to expand beyond Europe. With the arrival of the telephone, the charter of the ITU expanded beyond telegraphy, just as its charter would later be expanded to include radio transmission.

Governmental roles

Government plays several important roles in telecommunication, depending in large measure on whether the service provider is public or private. If it is public (that is, either a government agency or owned by the government), then government provides financing for the infrastructure. If it is private, the role of government falls more into motivating infrastructure development and regulation of private firms. Note that the term 'public carrier' refers to a carrier whose services are generally available to all, whether publicly or privately owned. One of the important roles of governmental and international organizations has been to finance the development of telecommunication infrastructures. This has ranged from special projects (as in the Morse example cited above) to complete infrastructure development, as with governmental Post, Telegraph and Telephone (PTT) organizations. Internationally, the World Bank and the International Monetary Fund (IMF) have become involved in the financial support of telecommunication infrastructure building in developing countries.

Regulation

In countries where the telecommunication service provider is private (an increasingly common occurrence), regulation is often necessary. Regulation is particularly important in situations where no viable competitor exists to prevent monopolistic pricing by the service provider. Governments must usually establish a credible regulatory capability as they look to privatize their telecommunication operators. The regulatory body must be independent of the service providers and serves the functions of preventing 'abusive' pricing, ensuring the economic viability of the service provider, and providing a stable legal and economic framework for telecommunication to enable the service providers to engage in long-term planning.

Regulation frequently takes the form of tariffs: A tariff defines a service as well as establishing the price of the service. As common carriers, many telecommunication service providers are obliged to apply the tariffs uniformly to all persons or parties requesting the service. Since the underlying cost of the service varies by customer, this averaging implies an implicit subsidy from the low cost-of-service customers to high cost-of-service customers.

As competition is introduced into telecommunication markets, these implicit subsidies (and hence the averaging strategy implicit in tariffs) become harder to sustain. This occurs because the relatively high-tariffed prices for low cost-of-service customers presents a market opportunity for new entrants. Regulation may also take the form of rules and standards. Unlike tariffs, which have explicitly economic subject-matter, rules and standards seek to restrict the behaviour of firms. Rules and standards can govern technical matters (radio broadcast, for example, and the ways in which different carriers must interconnect) or structural matters (for example, how firms must separate regulated business from non-regulated business, and which markets are open to competitive entry). Although these rules are often not explicitly economic, they can frequently have profound economic implications.

International regulations have been set forth by the ITU and tend to focus on technical standards and mechanisms for co-operation between interconnecting carriers. The ITU has not engaged in price regulation of service providers, although it has established a set of structures to facilitate the creation of international tariffs and periodic settlements between carriers.

The establishment and operation of transnational communication links poses some special problems. While the ITU provides useful frameworks to facilitate this, many of the details must be worked out through bilateral negotiations between the countries involved. While there is a significant precedent for most negotiations, special problems can sometimes arise. These include landing rights for cable or satellite systems; accounting and settlements rates and procedures; facilities ownership; and telecommunication market structure issues, such as public versus private and competitive versus monopoly. Governments have taken active roles in defining these issues, although there is a clear worldwide trend toward private ownership and competitive markets (and away from public ownership and monopoly service provision).

When telecommunication is provided by the government or by a government-owned firm, representation on international bodies and the status of the carriers is straightforward. With a privately owned carrier, or a multitude of privately owned carriers, this becomes more difficult. While the representation on international bodies, particularly the ITU, remains the same, the way in which international regulations are enforced and the way in which national policy vis-à-vis international telecommunication is made become more difficult. While each country with competitive, private carriers has developed different strategies for this, the general approach is relatively constant: private carriers with international links must agree to abide by ITU regulations by registering as a Registered Private Operating Agency (RPOA) and by collaborative development of public policies through national advisory councils of the foreign ministry.

Multinational corporations

Multinational corporations are often advanced users of a country's telecommunication infrastructure. These corporations normally do not have the goal of enhancing a country's infrastructure; rather, they are interested in the efficient operation of their global enterprise. Multinational corporations were most frequently the first users of technologies such as X.25, Frame Relay and EDI, for example. But multinational firms can have a bigger impact.

As a large and advanced user, a multinational can command significant investment by the public network service provider because the multinational offers a future stream of revenues to justify that investment, and also because it has the means and technology to bypass the public carrier, if necessary, to ensure that its communication needs are met. While the bypass threat can be mitigated to some extent by the use of 'landing rights' and licensing, the use of these measures may be detrimental to further investments by multinationals. Once the infrastructure investments are made, many users can take advantage of the advanced services, since it is unlikely that the multinational will consume the entire capacity of the carrier. The multinational, then, can provide a stimulus for infrastructure development that can assist a country in further economic development. From a public policy perspective, then, a multinational can pose significant challenges to the status quo and to public policy goals. The needs of multinationals have stimulated the move to privatization and the entry of competition as mechanisms to meet their needs.

The focused infrastructure investments needed to support a multinational's needs can lead to conflicts with social equity concerns inherent in universal service policy goals. This conflict is particularly acute if annual investments are fixed, requiring the carrier to defer other investments to meet the needs of the multinational user.

Telecommunication is a 'standards-intensive' industry by its very nature: Thus, an important role of governments and international organizations is to foster the establishment of standards. There are many ways in which standards may be set and many organizational structures within which standards may be developed. Originally the ITU, as a treaty organization, was created very much to serve the needs of public telecommunication networks, while ISO was more focused on meeting the needs of equipment, system and software manufacturers and vendors. The Internet Engineering Task Force (IETF), the body within which standards for the Internet are developed, is loosely organized and informal. The traditional distinctions between these organizations are blurring and a good deal of cooperation takes place among them.

The two most visible standard-setting organizations in the telecommunication business are the ITU and ISO; hence, only those will be profiled below. These profiles are very brief; more detailed information can be found on the World Wide Web.

International Telecommunications Union (ITU)

The ITU, a Specialized Agency of the UnitedNations, is the primary focus for international cooperation in telecommunication. As a treaty organization, the recommendations and regulations of the ITU carry considerable weight. It dates back to 1865, and became a Specialized Agency of the United Nations in 1947. In 1992, the ITU was reorganized, and has been aggressively pursuing procedural reforms to accelerate the development of technical standards. In general terms, the mission of the ITU is to facilitate international telecommunication, and its standards development activities are concentrated on fostering that mission. As a result, the ITU has been active in developing standards for radio transmission (and coordinating frequency usage), digital and analogue telephone systems, telegraph and telex, and selected data communications standards. In the domain of data communications, the focus has been on those standards of interest to public network operators, including X.25, Frame Relay and X.400.

Telecommunication standards are developed within the ITU-T. The actual work of standards development is not funded by the ITU; rather, the 'volunteers' who prepare the documents that define the standards are supported by telephone carriers, industrial organizations and other interested parties. The ITU provides a framework and organizational support for these activities.

International Standards Organization (ISO). Unlike the ITU, ISO is not a treaty organization. Its purpose is to achieve worldwide agreement on international standards - a purpose with a much larger scope than just telecommunication or information systems standards. For example, ISO sets standardsin areas such as Fire Safety, Plastics, and Information and Documentation. Unlike the ITU, ISO is a federation of national standards bodies, governmental or non-governmental. As a result, industry has a strong voice and the right to vote.

The Internet

In a remarkably short time, the Internet has evolved from an academic curiosity to a mass medium. It has been heralded as the basis of economic salvation for developing nations, as a new scholarly communications system and even as an entertainment alternative to television. However, the Internet has also thrown into relief controversial issues relating to censorship and freedom of expression, pornography and intellectual property rights that have profound ramifications for both individuals and nation-states. This chapter describes and seeks to explain the phenomenon that is the Internet.

The earliest experiments in what later became the Internet began in 1966 with the United States Department of Defense Advanced Research Projects Agency

(DARPA). The first nodes in the resultant ARPANET were created in 1969. In 1977, the TCP/IP (Transmission Control Protocol/Internet Protocol) protocols that underlay the Internet were demonstrated for the first time. In 1986, the National Science Foundation (NSF) created the first NSFNET backbone and allowed regional networks, mostly supporting universities, to feed into this backbone.

By 1990, the Internet was supporting commercial activities. Even after all this growth and development, the same basic TCP/IP protocols remain in use and still serve to unify the Internet. In March 1989, the first World Wide Web (WWW) proposal was elaborated and circulated at the European Laboratory for Particle Physics (CERN) in Geneva, Switzerland, and in November 1990 the first prototype Web browser was created.

Growth

The most comprehensive and regularly administered survey of Internet-connected computers, or hosts, is the Internet Domain Survey. The number of Internet hosts from 1981 to 1995, is based on this survey. From the data, it can be seen that the number of host computers on the Internet doubles approximately annually. Additional statistics on Internet growth are provided by the Internet Society, and Matrix Information and Directory Services. The number of computers on the World Wide Web, currently the most popular portion of the Internet, is doubling every four or five months. The number of electronic mail messages sent over the Internet is doubling approximately every year. As of January 1996, there were an estimated 9,472,000 host computers on the

Internet. International growth is highly variable. There is also considerable variation in Internet presence for different industry sectors.

A defining feature of the Internet is that no one person, company, government or organization has ultimate control. The Internet Society (ISOC), an international, non-governmental organization whose members consist of governments, corporations, individuals and not-for-profit organizations, co-ordinates many activities related to technical standards, globalization, administrative procedures, education and training, and scaling. The ISOC Board of Trustees is the governing body of the ISOC. The Internet Activities Board (IAB), a technical advisory group to ISOC, is responsible for oversight of Internet technical standards, for the standards-making process and for all protocols and architectures used on the Internet.

In addition, the IAB acts as a liaison with other national and international standards-making organizations, such as the International standards Organization (ISO) and the American National Standards Institute (ANSI), and publishes the Request for Comments (RFC) document series that effectively defines Internet standards and conventions.

The IAB and the Federal Networking Council (FNC) have delegated responsibility for coordinating the management and dissemination of unique Internet host computer numbers, domain names and other parameters to the Internet Assigned Numbers Authority (IANA) at the University of Southern California. The Internet Network Information Center (InterNIC), maintained by AT&T and Network Solutions, provides site, host, domain and personal directory services to the Internet.

Protocols and standards are researched and developed by the Internet Engineering Task Force (IETF), which also administers the overall Internet standards-making process. An open organization of network designers, vendors and researchers, the IETF, manages Internet standards through the RFC document series. The chair of the IETF, along with the area directors of the IETF, form the IESG (Internet Engineering Steering Group) that handles policy issues related to protocol research and development. RFCs, the official and published documents of the IETF (and thus the Internet), are divided into four different types: Standards Track, Informational, Experimental and Historic. Standards Track RFCs go through three phases: Proposed, Draft Standard and Standard.

Access

Access to the Internet is often divided into three classes, a trichotomy first proposed by Matrix Information and Directory Services: the Core Internet, consisting of those who can provide or distribute information over the Internet, the Consumer Internet, consisting of people who can receive information over the Internet, and the Matrix, consisting of users with access to electronic mail systems who can exchange mail with Internet users, including most proprietary, corporate e-mail systems. Until recently, the most common way to access the Internet was through a university or government agency. However, in the course of 1995, the number of hosts in the commercial domain exceeded the number of hosts in the educational domain for the first time.

Users with personal accounts generally access the Internet by dialling in with a modem, either through a commercial online service such as America Online, CompuServe or Prodigy, or directly to the Internet through a local Internet Service Provider (ISP), otherwise known as a Point of Presence (POP). These commercial services provide additional proprietary information not available on the Internet as well as Internet access. ISPs can range in size from a couple of simultaneous connections operating from an individual's home to large, national providers such as PSI in the United States or I-Way, Pipex, U-Net and Demon Internet in the United Kingdom. In developed nations, the telephone call to the ISP is most often a local call.

Almost all the United Kingdom and much of the United States are covered locally by ISPs. Recently, ISPs have also begun to appear in other countries. In the United States, the Telecommunications Act of 1996 makes it likely that telephone companies, both local Regional Bell Operating Companies (RBOCs) and long-distance carriers, will begin offering Internet connectivity as a standard service. France Telecom has also announced intentions to provide a consumer internet service, one that will include (for an extra fee) access to its existing Minitel service. If this happens, it is unlikely that local ISPs will be able to survive without offering significant added value.

In addition, some users have access to limited parts of the Internet (often just electronic mail) through local computer bulletin board systems (BBS) or community networks ('freenets'). An alternative means of connection is through what is called a 'shell account', in which a user dials into a remote computer connected to the Internet. Users in this case may have limited access to certain Internet services (e-mail, Usenet newsgroups, and even the World Wide Web), although they generally do not have access to graphics or many of the more advanced services. The advantage of this type of account, however, is that it requires only a low-end computer and a slow modem, and it is particularly popular in developing countries, where higher-end equipment is often unavailable.

Pricing models for Internet access are varied, and have been the subject of much study. The economics of the Internet in terms of the characteristics of its primary underlying technologies, leased lines and routers (computers used to direct data traffic), both of which are subject to large economies of scale. Additional factors to be taken into account are the continually declining costs of the computer hardware and the statistical multiplexing techniques used to combine the traffic from different sources into a steady average traffic stream, both of which serve to drive down marginal costs.

Internet economics from the perspective of congestion control. They compare fixed-rate access to the Internet with the 'tragedy of the commons', wherein there is no penalty for increased use, resulting in 'over grazing' of the resource (for example, excessive cross-posting of messages). They posit an Internet costing model based on: incremental packet cost, social cost of delay to others, network infrastructure fixed costs, incremental cost of connecting an additional user, and cost to expand network capacity.

Most authors, even those in favour of a more use-based Internet pricing model, agree that some subsidies for civic, educational and not-for-profit use are required. The provision of subsidies to schools and public libraries for Internet access. Subsidies are not peculiar to the United States, however. For example, in Tarragona, Spain, TINET (Tarragona Internet) has begun offering users free basic Internet service (electronic mail and Usenet news), and below-market rate full Internet service, and the Peruvian Scientific Network (RCP), seeded with monies from the United Nations Development Programme (UNDP), is providing subsidized Internet access and training to the public.

A Web site or page can also be the level of economic analysis. Thus far, relatively few sites charge for the content they provide, with the information either being funded through advertising or provided as a loss-leader to entice the user to purchase a more complete version of the product. The Fourth World Wide Web Survey revealed that the number of people unwilling to pay anything for access to Web sites had increased to 31.8% from 22.6% in the previous survey.

Internet services

Internet services are combinations of protocols and software programs that allow people to use the Internet in different ways. A number of genres have emerged over the lifetime of the Internet, and most are still being used today, albeit in various incarnations. Usenet is a distributed network of computers, predating the Internet but now running almost entirely on the Internet infrastructure, that exchanges messages via a set of agreed-upon protocols in collections of messages called newsgroups. These newsgroups can be thought of as electronic discussion groups, and are arranged in hierarchies. There are seven top-level international hierarchies of newsgroups, called comp (for computer-related discussions and information), sci (for the sciences), soc (for sociocultural issues), rec (for hobbies and recreational activities), news (for activities related to

Usenet itself), talk (for debate-oriented activities) and misc (for activities not fitting into one of the existing categories or spanning categories). In addition to the global hierarchies, there also exist local, regional and national hierarchies (de for Germany, in for Indiana, etc.). Finally, there are alternative hierarchies that are carried by some news servers, including the anarchic alt hierarchy, which has been the subject of controversy owing in part to the sexually explicit nature of some of its newsgroups. While there is no central Usenet authority, a number of accepted rules and procedures have evolved that users and news server administrators abide by in the maintenance of Usenet newsgroups for the seven major global hierarchies. These procedures include calls for discussion about the creation of new newsgropus, calls for voting on the creation of such newsgropus, and protocols for the collection and counting of votes and subsequent action.

Gopher, developed at the University of Minnesota in the United States, was the first multi-media-oriented network navigation tool. Designed to simplify network navigation for the user by allowing providers to present their information in the form of navigable hierarchical menus, Gopher, and its companion Internet search index, VERONICA, played a major role in increasing the accessibility of the Internet to the nontechnical user. Although many Gopher-based servers still exist, Gopher has been largely superseded by the World Wide Web, which duplicates and significantly enhances its functionality.

Undoubtedly, the most significant Internet service is the World Wide Web - often referred to as the multimedia portion of the Internet. The World Wide Web is based on the concepts of hypertext and hypermedia.

Information available via the World Wide Web is provided in the form of hypermedia pages, which look like pages from a magazine, combining graphics and text, but with the added feature that the user can follow links provided by the author to other documents. Users view these hypermedia pages with the aid of software programs known as Web browsers. While the first widely available Web browser was Mosaic, more recently Netscape Navigator has become the browser of choice for most people. Browsers on the World Wide Web access Web servers via HTTP, or HyperText Transport Protocol. Information on the Web is generally marked up with HyperText Markup Language (HTML), a subset of the Standard Generalized Markup Language (SGML). HTML provides facilities for the incorporation of text, graphics, sound, video and hypertext links into Web-based documents, as well as document formatting. To provide documents over the Web, information providers mark up these documents using HTML codes (or tags) and make them available via an HTTP server.

HTML is a continuously evolving standard, and HTML 2.0 is the currently accepted version, supported by almost every browser. HTML 3.0 is currently under discussion, though many Web browsers have already implemented some of its features. Some browser developers, notably Netscape and Microsoft, have implemented nonstandard features, and a major discussion item among Web service developers is the degree to which these features should be utilized.

Most recent developments in Internet service are intended to fit within the World Wide Web and HTML framework, which has proven remarkably extensible and flexible. Virtual Reality Modeling Language (VRML) is a technology used to represent three-dimensional interactive objects and scenes.

2

Information and Communication Technologies: A Social Development Approach

Beyond economic growth, which is an engine and not an end in itself, development is first and foremost social; it is also intimately linked to peace, human rights, democratic governance, environment, and last but not least, the culture and life styles of the people. The United Nations Development Programme (UNDP), on its side, launched in 1990, together with its Human Development Report, the concept of human development, which has become the 'leading alternative to the view of development equated exclusively with economic growth. Human development focuses on people. One result of this change in focus is that the eradication of poverty has become a multidimensional activity.

Poverty is considered to be more than a lack of material well-being. It also reflects poor health and education, deprivation in knowledge and communication, inability to exercise human and political rights and the absence of dignity, confidence and self-respect. ICTs play a prominent role in this broader conception of poverty. They provide important tools for the improvement of health and education, offer new channels for the diffusion of knowledge and create physical and virtual spaces for social communication. This human approach does not ignore the importance of economic growth and productivity, but addresses the question of how economic performance relates to human empowerment and thus asks whether such growth is equitable and sustainable.

Human development implies that people's capabilities are enhanced and their lives enriched. In the annual reports of the UNDP, human development is defined as the 'process of enlarging people's choices'. This is achieved 'by expanding human capabilities and functionings. At all levels of development the three essential capabilities for human development are for people to lead long and healthy lives, to be knowledgeable and to have access to the resources needed for a decent standard of living'.

The essential features of human development are:

— equity in access to vital resources and capabilities

— sustainability of resources and institutions

— acquisition and distribution of knowledge for human empowerment

— people's participation

Attempts to measure the impact of ICTs on the economies of industrialized and developing countries encounter severe problems of statistical classification and data availability Data are not always reliable . They may be unclear or use different definitions, classification schemes are contested and some data are protected as company property. An important reason for the difficulty in measuring productivity is that ICTs are used to produce an intermediate good or product, information. The value of information in use varies dramatically depending upon the context.

A further complication for a full global assessment is that most of the developing countries still have to begin the process of harnessing ICTs to their development goals . Another problem is that ICT deployment and economic growth have a dialectical relationship so that there are no unilateral causal links. Economic growth may be partly the result of the growth in the use of ICTs, but then the proliferation of ICTs is itself dependent upon the availability of economic resources. If the definition of development is extended beyond mere economic growth, the assessment is complicated even further.

Across all industries, there has been a strong growth of investments in ICT applications. Spending on ICT equipment as part of overall spending on business equipment has grown dramatically in most industrial countries. In the United States, for example, such spending rose from less than 5% in 1960 to over 45% by 1996 and if the current trend continues the figure could be over 50% in 2000.

According to an estimate of the United States Department of Commerce (the United States Bureau of the Census and Bureau of Economic Analysis for 1990-1995) in 1998, the American ICT-industry generated $683,000 million. In some industrial countries ICT-related activities produce a growing share of the Gross Domestic Product (GDP).

In the United States, the ICT-industry accounted for almost 8% of the GDP in 1997 and was responsible for over 12% of GDP growth. In the Organisation for Economic Development and Co-operation (OECD) countries, the ICT market sector generally accounts for 15% to 25% of current real economic growth. Investments in the telecommunications sector are an important indicator of the economic significance of ICTs. Worldwide investments in telecommunication rose from $115,000 million in 1990 to $152,000 million in 1995. These investments have often been linked to the privatization of public telecommunication operators (PTOs). The privatization schemes introduced in a number of countries have raised considerable funds.

The ICT industry encompasses the manufacturing of telecommunications equipment, computers, semiconductors and other electronic equipment, the provision of telecommunications services, computer services and software. It is the world's most important and fastest-growing industry. Of the fifty largest companies in the world, ten are ICT companies. They account for 17.5% of the total revenue of the fifty largest companies, for 23% of the total profits and for 26% of the total number of employees. In 1997, four ICT companies, General Electric, Microsoft, NTT and Intel, were among the ten largest companies in the world in terms of market value. In the same year three ICT companies, General Electric, Intel, and International Business Machines (IBM), were among the ten most profitable companies in the world.

Telecommunications, semiconductors and computers are among the high growth industries in the emerging-market economies. Among the 200 top companies in these economies, twenty-two are telecommunications market operators and ten are electronics products manufacturers.

ICTs are affected by a great deal of merger activity. The largest transactions of 1998 include the SBC Communications merger with Ameritech for $272,400 million, AT&T with Telecommunications Inc. (TCI) for $48,000 million, Worldcom with MCI Comm for $37,000 million, Northern Telecom with Bay Networks for $9,000 million, and Alcatel with Digital Service Corporation (DSC) for $4,400 million. There is high degree of concentration in this industry. In the telecommunications equipment market, for example, 50% of all sales are controlled by only five companies. In the market for public telephone switching equipment, five firms (Alcatel, Siemens, Lucent, Ericsson and Nortel) control 76% of all activity. The major companies that carry the bulk of international telephone traffic have formed global alliances. These are:

— Leading companies in the ICT industry, 1997;

— Concert Communications Company (of which 75% is owned by British Telecom and 25% by WorldCom-MCI) with revenues in 1995 of $37,300 million;

— Global One (Deutsche Telekom, 10% + France Telecom, 10% + Sprint USA) with 1995 revenues of $88,500 million;

— Unisource (Telia of Sweden, Royal KPN of the Netherlands, the Swiss PTT and Telefonica in Spain) with 1995 revenues of $37,400 million;

— Cable & Wireless (a United Kingdom based company with interests in over 25 public telephone operators

(PTOs) throughout the world) with revenues in 1995 of $8,500 million.

These four alliances are responsible for some 30% of worldwide telecommunication services revenues. Another example of concentration is provided by Internet traffic. The world's largest Internet Service provider (ISP) is UUNET, which is the subsidiary of the company WorldCom (that merged with MCI), responsible for over 50% of the Internet backbone traffic. One company, Netscape, controls 74% of the market for World Wide Web navigators, with 8% for America Online and 4% for Microsoft (Forrester Research).

The ICT market is growing rapidly and expanding globally. The top ten companies in the manufacturing of telecommunication equipment derive an average 61% of their revenues from sales abroad. These are Motorola (United States), Alcatel (France), Lucent (United States), Siemens (Germany), Ericsson (Sweden), NEC (Japan), Nortel (Canada), Nokia (Finland), Fujitsu (Japan), and Bosch (Germany). Most analysts expect a further growth of global sales since the domestic markets in many countries are either too small or already saturated. From various trade figures, it can be estimated that the share of the ICT industry in the world economy ranges from between 10% to 15% of total world trade.

In several ICT sectors the world market shows rapid growth rates. The market for computer hardware and software, for example, grew at about 15% annually in the 1990-1995 period. In the same period, the average growth rate for total world trade was 8%. In 1997, worldwide revenues in the telecommunications industry were nearly $600,000 million. Some analysts expect this figure to grow to $1,400,000 million by the year 2000.

The value of total imports in the world trade of computer equipment grew by 67% from $87,500 million in 1992 to $145,500 million in 1996. The value of total exports grew by 75% from $73,000 million in 1992 to $127,000 million in 1996 (Comtrade, United Nations Statistics Division). The market for personal computers (PCs) is still growing and may reach a sales figure of over $250,000 million in 2000. There is also rapid growth in the world market for computer software, which in 1996 generated $109 , 3 00 million in revenues.

In the world trade of telecommunication equipment the value of total exports grew by 68% from $65,000 million in 1992 to $108,000 million in 1996. The value of total imports grew by 58% from $66,000 million in 1992 to $104,000 million in 1996. Growth rates in this sector are linked to the worldwide increase in the number of telephone lines. The growth from 519 million lines in 1990 to 693 million lines in 1995 represents an average growth rate of 6.8% per year.

In 1995, 45 million new fixed telephone lines were added and 33 million people became new subscribers to mobile communications. In fact, the strongest growth rates are in the mobile communication market, particularly in the United States and Japan. In the OECD countries in 1996-67, the contribution of mobile communications to overall telecommunication services revenues amounted to some 12% and the number of subscribers doubled. In 1990, the worldwide trading of telecommunications services generated some $377,000 million. This figure increased in 1996 to over $600,000 million.

Largely as a result of the further internationalization of transnational corporations and increases in the volume of travel, this sector of the market continues to show very high growth rates. There is an ever-growing demand for telecommunication services around the world and thus for the building and renovation of networks.

The total value of exports in the world trade of audio and video recording equipment grew by 23% from $18,000 million in 1992 to $21,000 million in 1996. The total value of imports grew by 6% from $17,000 million in 1992 to $18,000 million in 1996.

Trade balance

According to data from the International Telecomunications Union (ITU), the developed countries represent some 70% of overall telecommunication equipment exports, showing a $9 billion trade surplus. Particularly striking is the shift from a trade deficit for the USA in 1990 to a trade surplus of $3.2 billion in 1995. Over 100 developing countries produce no exports at all. They are obliged to import and thus show trade deficits that in 1995 exceeded $10,000 million.

For most developing countries, the obvious problem is lack of capital for imports, since low overall income means that local telecommunications generate minimal revenues. The profits in national telecommunications operation are, without exception, found in international traffic, but the financial gains from overseas services do not benefit the national telecommunications carrier. For political and other reasons, many countries decide not to reinvest a sufficient share of this income in the expansion and upgrading of telecommunication facilities.

Moreover, there is growing competition in the provision of international telecommunications services and strong pressures to lower rates on busy routes. Foreign investments in telecommunications have been stimulated by the privatization of former national public telecommunication operators as part of the worldwide trend toward deregulation that emerged during the 1980s. In the 1984-96 period the 44 PTOs that were privatized raised in total a sum of $159,000 million. Almost one third of the financing came from foreign investments.

Electronic Commerce

The increasing economic importance of ICTs is also linked to the growth of electronic commerce. Although for the moment electronic commerce is still a factor of limited economic significance, with revenues of approximately $26,000 million in 1998, this figure is expected to exceed the trillion dollar mark in the early 21st century.

Since it is difficult to measure precisely the economic significance of electronic commerce. Several of its important features, such as easy access to data, cannot be quantified, and reliable and comprehensive statistics are not yet available; this uncertainty leads to widely varying estimates. The OECD definition of electronic commerce refers to commercial transactions that take place through open networks, like the Internet. These transactions are both business to business and business to consumers. The growing number of people around the world connected to the Internet have begun to develop a digital economy.

In cyberspace, consumers can purchase flowers, shirts, jeans, books, compact disks (CDs), tickets, hotel reservations, skin care products, pornography, kitchen equipment and household consumer goods. World Wide Web sales grew approximately from $8,000 million in 1994 to over $45,000 million in 1998. According to various analysts in Business Week, digital trade could grow from $1,200 million in 1998 to $65,000 million over the next three years. Other forecasters propose even higher figures, for instance in the travel industry, book and music sales and financial services. Electronic sales of software also hold enormous growth potential.

Whatever the precise significance and validity of the forecasts, the general expectation predicts formidable growth in this sector of the global economy. Most analysts observe that this will be mainly business-to-business trading. Expectations of growth in the business-to-consumer trade are based on the assumption that on-line trading will lower production, and thus distribution, costs by up to 10% of total sales. Some 50% of this reduction of costs may be used to lower consumer prices thus stimulating further purchases by consumers.

Electronic trading via the Internet is in fact the successor to the Electronic Data Interchange (EDI) that is already used by many companies. EDI is the exchange of electronic documents in goods trading and financial services and usually operates within closed Value Added Networks (VANs).

EDI is expensive because complicated software applications have to be installed for each new trading partner and flexibility is limited because invoices and orders must be exchanged in fixed standard formats. The Internet facilitates the exchange of electronic data by accepting many different formats. However, many of the big EDI users see EDI as more reliable than current Internet traffic. In the United States at present, the volume of EDI-traffic is some fourteen times greater than that of Internet traffic.

Many analysts expect that in the years ahead this ratio will change, first to a more equal distribution between EDI and Internet transactions and later to a definite advance for the Internet. This situation will be reinforced by the rate at which companies begin to share their 'intranets' with more trading partners and thus create 'extranets'.

Controlling Access to Cyberspace

An increasingly important part of all commercial activity on the digital market is geared toward the control over access to cyberspace. The gates that provide access to the World Wide Web - the so-called web-portals - have become crucial targets in the struggle for dominance in this market. In 1998 a veritable 'portal-fever' emerged as more and more companies sought to secure a piece of the expected profits.

In June 1998 the media giant Walt Disney announced it would spend $70 million for the purchase of 43% of the stock in the search engine Infoseek. In 1998, the American National Broadcasting Company (NBC) invested $165 million for the purchase of the online service Snap! from van Cnet Inc. Time-Warner and News Corp. began to develop their own web portals.

Manufacturers of personal computers, vendors of operating systems, producers of browsers, telecommunications operators, Internet Service Providers, search engines, the big producers of information and entertainment are among the many contenders in this field. Recent acquisitions or investments among the various companies involved in cyberspace illustrate the high level of competition in this area. In 1997, Microsoft bought a 5% participation in Apple Computer for $150 million. As part of the deal, Microsoft insisted that Apple Macintosh computers be delivered with the Microsoft 'browser', Explorer. In 1998 Compaq Computer acquired Digital Equipment in a deal valued at $9,600 million. The combined revenues are estimated at around $38,000 million. WorldCom controls 60% of worldwide Internet traffic and can be seen as a major gatekeeper of access to lines and networks.

In September 1997, America Online (AOL) acquired Compuserve through a complicated deal that made WorldCom the owner of Compuserve's infrastructure. WorldCom paid $1,200 million to H&R Block (Columbus, Ohio) for the purchase of Compuserve. The subscribers to Compuserve were sold to AOL. Through this deal AOL became the largest ISP on the European market with 1.5 million subscribers. On the world market, AOL has some 12 million subscribers.

The ISPs provide access to the services on the Internet and exercise considerable control over access to cyberspace. Some of them conclude agreements with the search engines. Provider MCI, for example, concluded a deal with Yahoo! in order to guide clients to the Web page of this particular search engine. The world market of ISPs is concentrated. If interest in the Web continues to grow, ISPs are likely to allow certain websites to purchase a right of 'priority'. This would mean that if too many clients browse the Web at one time, customers of the privileged sites will have priority and have to wait less time than others. There is also market concentration in this area and many linkages among the players.

ICTs and Employment

In 1996 in the United States, over 7 million people were employed in ICT firms and in ICT-related jobs. This means that ICT-related employment represented over 6% of overall employment. The indications are that this growth will continue. The picture is, however, very different when different economies and market sectors are considered. In several state economies, there has been an increase of employment in such ICT-related professions as technicians, programmers, operators, assemblers and analysts.

Growth of employment opportunities is particularly strong in the software sector. In California's Silicon valley, over 50,000 new jobs were created during 1996 with higher incomes than the national industry averages. However, in the sector that manufactures the technologies themselves, jobs decreased.

The creation of new employment is often related to various uses of ICT, for example in new service applications in banking, shopping, education, health and business services. The development of networks combined with the lowering of communication costs has stimulated the growth of 'teleworking'. This means that people work from home and use telecommunication services. The fastest growth is generally expected in 'telecommuting' where people work alternately at home and at the office.

The Internet could play a major role in creating employment for the design, maintenance and management of sites on the World Wide Web. The growth of electronic commerce initially raised concerns about implications for the labour market, but there is also the expectation that few jobs will really be lost since companies will continue to use traditional forms of commerce along with digital trading. When digital trading finally predominates, some jobs will be lost, but new ones requiring new skills will also have been created. The overall picture is characterized by contradictions. Information-related service jobs are associated with the dislocation of family and community life and threats to the health of workers, especially of women. On the other, new types of employment and modes of work organization can be highly beneficial leading to improved quality of life and greater economic resources.

There is some empirical evidence that automation eliminates jobs, but there is also evidence that automation creates new jobs. What remains uncertain is the eventual balance. The notion of a single standard impact is very inadequate and it is preferable to look at plural impacts. The skills implications of ICTs are varied and are related to differences in socio-economic, cultural and political environments. Different countries will choose different ICT-applications in order to reap different benefits from technological development. It is too early to foresee how all these factors will operate. The observation that in the affluent economies more and more employees use ICT applications in their daily work is generally uncontested. By and large, ICTs are used by some 50% of the workforce in the industrial nations.

ICTs and Economic Productivity

The processing capacity of ICTs doubles every two years, but this is not matched by growth in economic productivity. There are indications of a real ICT contribution to overall economic growth, although no definite assessment is possible. In his testimony to Congress, US Federal Reserve Board Chairman Alan Greenspan pointed to increasing growth rates in productivity for the American economy and stated that: 'The dramatic improvements in computing power and communication and information technology appear to have been a major force behind this beneficial trend'. Other analysts raise serious doubts about such a causal link between ICT power and productivity.

Of the world's total investment in capital goods, 50% concerns computers and peripherals. Yet expected growth in productivity has not materialized. During the period 1970-90 white collar productivity remained stagnant at around 0.9% per year and improved in the early 1990s to 1.3% - a low figure despite the announcement by Fortune magazine that 'the productivity payoff arrives'. It is not clear at present what factors cause this ICT-paradox. One possible explanation refers to the criteria that are used for the measurement of economic productivity. Another factor may also be the inadequate way in which organizations adapt to the use of ICTs. It could also be that what looks like an unexplainable delay is in fact the normal time lag needed before new technologies can lead to higher levels of productivity.

ICTs are 'synergetic' technologies and their growth therefore leads to growth in other sectors of the economy. They create an infrastructure around their products and services, similar to that of car technology earlier in the century. As with the transition from manual power to mechanization techniques and later to electromechanical innovations, today's shift towards the pervasive application of ICTs has given rise to a range of new industries such as software production, processing services, time-sharing facilities, semiconductor manufacturing, database management or electronic publishing.

This potential for new economic productivity requires an educational infrastructure that teaches the knowledge and skills required for ICT-related occupations. Although there has been a considerable increase in ICT teaching in many schools and universities around the world, new multimedia tools are still widely underused or used only to supplement conventional teaching methods. There is also a lack of solid and creative training materials that cater for the specific needs of the developing countries.

The economic benefits that may accrue from the development and the deployment of ICTs are unequally distributed throughout the world. There seems to be general agreement in scientific literature and in public policy statements that the ICT gap between the developed and developing countries is widening and will be a major obstacle to the integration of all countries into the so-called Global Information Society.

The seriousness of the ICT gap is clearly demonstrated by figures on the world distribution of telephones. In 1996 there were 743.66 million main telephone lines in the world. Europe (274.23 million), the United States (170 . 5 7 million) and Japan (61.53 million) represent 68% of this total, compared with 1.8% in Africa. The density of telephone lines per 100 inhabitants is also very unequally distributed. Whereas the world average is 12.88 lines per 100 inhabitants, Europe provides 34.6, the United States 63.9, Japan 48.9 and Africa 1.85. In early 1997, some 62% of the world's main telephone lines were installed in 23 affluent countries, which account for only 15% of the world's population. Over 950 million households in the world (65% of the total) were equipped with a telephone. Another indicator of this gap is the revenue from telecommunication services, which reached a world total of $620,000 million in 1996. Europe, the United States and Japan benefited from 77% of these revenues, while Africa received a mere 1.5%. Investments in the telecommunication sector show a similar distribution. In 1996 the world total was worth $166,000 million. Europe, the United States and Japan are responsible for 67% of these investments and Africa for 1.7%.

Total ICT equipment installation reveals highly uneven geographical distribution. The estimated number of PCs in the world in 1996 stood at 234,200,000. The share for Europe (72,864,000), the United States (96,600,000) and Japan (16,100,000) was 79%, while for Africa it was only 1.3%, representing 0 . 6 4 computers per 100 inhabitants. The world average for that year was 4.6 computers per 10 0 inhabitants. Far above this average are the figures for Europe, 9.6, the United States, 36.2, and Japan, 12.8. Of all the 47,972,000 fax machines operating in the world in 1996, Europe was using 10,942,500, the United States 17,000,000, and Japan 14,300,000. These figures combined represent 88%, in contrast with the 0.5% in use in Africa. Of the total number of television sets in the world in 1996, Europe, the United States and Japan possessed 47% while Africa possessed only 3%.

At the present time the worldwide distribution of ICT resources is enormously unequal. In terms of availability, accessibility, and affordability of equipment and services as well as the mastery of technical and managerial skills, there are great disparities not only between affluent and developing countries, but also among different social groups within all countries. A very problematic factor is that these disparities, rather than diminishing, are growing throughout the world.

Gender inequity

A particularly skewed worldwide distribution of ICT resources and use concerns women. An immediate problem is the fact that ICT skills are linked almost completely to literacy and 'it seems likely that the vast majority of the illiterate population will be excluded from the emerging knowledge societies'. This situation particularly affects women, since around the world illiteracy rates for women are higher than for men. In the developed world, a large majority of the population is literate, and most devices ensuring user-machine communication hardware and software - therefore reflect reading or writing capabilities.

ICTs could have developed devices based on sound, touch, images or symbols which do not require literacy, but markets are the driving force for technological developments, and the needs of illiterates in the developing world were, and still are, completely ignored. In terms of sharing ICT knowledge, women are also disadvantaged, since their numbers in enrolment for science and technology education lag far behind the figures for male enrolment. In 1990, the percentages of women enrolled in science and technology at the university level in Africa were 10%, in Latin America 40%, in Western Europe 32%, in Eastern Europe less than 30% and in the Asia/Pacific region 34%.

ICTs offer new forms of communication that may enable women to break through their often isolated social situation. They also create new opportunities of employment for women in jobs that require new skills. However, the technologies themselves will not achieve this. The full use of opportunities that are in principle created by the deployment of ICTs will depend upon social variables such as cultural factors, class and age. Robust policies are needed for the ICTs to have a beneficial impact on women's lives.

In the emerging 'knowledge societies' access to communication is becoming the key tool for social inclusion'. In most developing countries women are disadvantaged in terms of scientific and technological literacy, in terms of opportunities for education and training for the acquisition of technical skills, and in terms of real access to information and knowledge.

The ICT rush

In the 1980s, the expectation that innovations in telecommunications and computer technologies would improve industrial performance and increase economic productivity in the industrialized nations became firmly established among the leader of the developing countries. The common position that emerged was that ICTs would allow them to leapfrog over the industrialization of their economies into a post-industrial society. Countries began to launch policies and programmes to acquire a share in international satellite communications and transborder data flow networks. In many countries, however, concern arose that ICTs might entail serious social risks, such as a potential for cultural colonialism, the replacement of jobs by machines, and the erosion of individual privacy and national sovereignty.

Towards the end of the 1980s these fears seemed to have abated. A new phase began in the 1990s, characterized by a very strong fear of being left behind and cut off from the emerging global digital highway system. The general belief seems to be that without adequate access to the system, countries cannot hope to be economically competitive in world trade.

In many developing countries, the 'digital rush' is on to ensure connections with the electronic networks for trade, finance, transport and science. This phenomenon has been inspired by the obvious benefits that digital information and communication technologies - at least in principle - seem to offer. Educational facilities can be improved by providing distance learning and on-line library access.

Electronic networking has also been used to improve the quality of health services by providing remote access to the best diagnostic and healing practices and cutting costs in the process. Digital technologies for remote resource sensing can provide early warning to areas vulnerable to seismic disturbances or identify land suitable for crop cultivation.

Computer technology can contribute to the development of flexible, decentralized and small-scale industrial production. Thus the competitive position of local manufacturing and service industries can be improved. In Singapore, Brazil and Hong Kong the introduction of computer-aided manufacturing (CAM) technologies has been very successful in small-scale industries.

The World Commission on Environment and Development, in its report Our Common Future suggests that 'new technologies in communication, information, and process control allow the establishment of small-scale, decentralized, widely dispersed industries, thus reducing the levels of pollution and other impacts on the local environment'.

The currently available computer-communication technologies make it fairly easy for PC users around the world to create a public sphere in 'cyberspace'. Personal computers, modems and telephone lines are being used to establish new global communities. Organizations in developing countries find it increasingly possible to join these forms of horizontal, non-hierarchical exchange that have already demonstrated their ability to counter censorship and misinformation.

Groups of all types, from ecological movements, human rights activists, farmers, senior citizens, to the Zapatistas and the groups attending the Women's summit in Beijing, have made impressive use of the new, fast, reliable and effective networks of communication. The combination of telecommunication technologies with desktop publishing software has created new opportunities for even the smallest action group to disseminate its messages across the globe with relative ease and at minimal expense.

In the late 1980s and early 1990s, various aid projects introduced electronic information systems into rural health services (India), agricultural extension projects (Peru), infrastructural development (Pakistan), or energy management (Malaysia). In some developing countries, special computer training courses have been developed in schools and colleges (Sri Lanka).

The growing ICT-demand in developing countries can be seen in the long waiting lists for telephone connections, the increase in cellular systems and the rapidly expanding numbers of Internet users. To meet this demand, more and more developing countries have placed the ICTs at the centre of national agendas for social and economic development.

There are plans in many developing nations to enhance telecommunications infrastructures in order to facilitate participation in world markets. The planned increase in telephone lines over the next five years in developing countries represents a need for $200,000 million in investments, which it is expected will be provided largely through a massive inflow of foreign capital.

Human development challenges

Human development is forcing policy makers to face the complex challenges of equity of access with respect to vital resources and capabilities, the sustainability of resources and institutions, the acquisition and distribution of knowledge for human empowerment and people's participation. The reality of the widening gap in digital capacity raises the serious concern that the poorer countries may not be able to overcome the financial and technical obstacles now limiting their access to the digital technologies.

In early 1995 the concern about the ICT-gap inspired many public and private donor institutions to propose plans for the elimination of digital disparity. For example, the World Bank established the Information for Development Program to assist developing countries with their integration into the global information economy. In the same year, the ITU established World Tel, an ambitious project to generate private investments for bridging the telecommunications gap in the world by developing basic infrastructures. WorldTel aims to establish 40 million telephone connections in developing countries over the next ten years, which will require a minimal investment of $1,000 million.

The equitable sharing of communication infrastructures (the electronic highways systems created by carriers such as satellites, cables, fixed lines and mobile transmissions), computing capacity (computers, peripherals, networks), information resources (databases, libraries), and ICT-literacy (intellectual and social capabilities to deploy ICT in beneficial ways) will require an enormous effort from the international community.

Massive investments are required for the renovation, upgrading and expansion of networks in developing countries, for programmes to transfer knowledge and for ICT skill training, in particular for women. In 1985, the Maitland Commission estimated that an annual investment of $12,000 million would be needed to achieve the goal of simple, universal access to a telephone early in the 21st century.

To attract private funding, countries will have to liberalize their ICT markets and adopt measures in favour of competition. In this context the World Bank has recommended the creation of investor-friendly business environments, the protection of investments and security for repatriating revenues. When public companies are privatized there may be losses in revenues as a result of the change in service charges or severance payments. The World Bank is therefore proposing to finance the adjustment costs of the adoption of liberalization schemes in individual countries.

The World Bank's policies are characterized by a strong emphasis on economic growth and a key role for the private sector. The expectation is that, in a sufficiently free market, economic growth will also benefit the poorer sector of society. In this context the contribution of the ICTs is to provide the essential infrastructure for economic development. This position bypasses the question raised earlier, as to whether the deployment of ICTs does indeed lead to growth in economic productivity and, if so, whether such growth will be equitably distributed.

The governance of ICTs is in fact left to freely operating private entrepreneurs. The basic assumption is that a country's telecommunication infrastructure can be managed by private companies and that, whenever parts of the network are unprofitable, the state will provide the public means to ensure that no citizen is disenfranchised. There is some debate about the expectation that private funding will create worldwide equity in the access to and use of ICT resources. It appears in any case that the international community and national governments of affluent countries need to bear in mind that problems stem not only from a lack of financial resources but also from a lack of political will.

Creating adequate access to ICT resources worldwide should not be a problem in a world economy with income amounting to roughly $22 trillion. The core issue is that expenditures for development assistance represent only $55,000 million and thus a mere 0.25% of this income. The annual costs for all developing countries for adding one thousand million telephone lines, subsidizing over 600 million households that cannot afford basic telephone charges, providing PCs and access to the Internet for schools over a period of ten years could represent from $80,000 to $100,000 million. This is not a prohibitive level of funding.

It represents about 11% of the world's annual military expenditure, about 22% of total annual spending on narcotic drugs, and is comparable with the annual expenditure on alcoholic drinks in Europe alone. For a variety of political and economic reasons, many donor governments are presently reducing budgets for financing ICT-development. Between 1990 and 1995, multilateral lending for telecommunications decreased from $1,253 million to $967 million. Bilateral aid for telecommunications decreased from $1,259 million in 1990 to $800 million in 1995. Financial obstacles are, however, not the only concern. The transfer of ICTs also raises questions about their appropriateness and about the capacity of the recipient countries to make the best use of them.

Over the past few decades the prevailing international policies on technology transfer have placed formidable obstacles in the process of reducing North-South technology gaps; the present discussion on the ICT-gap provides no convincing evidence that the technology owners will change their attitudes and policies towards the international transfer of technology. There is no indication that current restrictive business practices, constraints on the ownership of knowledge, and rules on intellectual property rights that are adverse to developing country interests are radically changing, and there are no realistic prospects that the relations between ICT-rich and ICT-poor countries will change in the near future.

The question must be raised as to whether there can be any serious reduction of the ICT disparity, given the realities of the present international economic order. It may well be an illusion to think that the ICT-poor countries could catch up or keep pace with progress among countries in the Northern hemisphere, where the rate of technological development is very high and is supported by considerable resources. This is not to say that poor countries should not try to upgrade their ICT-systems. They should, however, not act with the unrealistic expectation that those who are ahead are planning to wait for them. The situation may improve for the poorer countries, but the disparity will not go away.

In most countries, the problems concerning access to ICTs are handled through public policies based on an already defined technological environment. Developing countries thus find it difficult to assess what digital technologies would be appropriate for their specific development strategies. A problem compounding this situation is that in many cases 'peripheral states seem to have no disinterested non-governmental organizations to advise them on telecommunication technology and the social objectives of regulation that would safeguard those interests that private profit will not meet. Without adequate regulatory intervention to ensure accountability to the general public, market forces that respond to those groups with purchasing power are bound to generate unequal development'.

Most developing countries lack the capacity to identify appropriate digital technologies, and, to make matters worse, there is also a critical absence of co-ordination of 'digital' policies among the developing countries themselves. It is essential to recognize that planning for the adoption and deployment of digital technologies can no longer be a local affair. Global negotiations, such as the recent General Agreement on Tariffs and Trade (GATT) Uruguay Round of Multilateral Trade Negotiations, heavily affect national technology plans, while the processes of globalization.

Information and communication technologies and social processes (in trade, finance, culture, etc.) determine the playing field for local actors. As a result, local planning has to take into account the effects of global forces, possible only when planners in the periphery pool resources and mobilize a constituency that counteracts the Northern dominance in global planning. Since today's globalization process is largely determined by Northern forces, 'many developing countries do not obtain a fair share of the benefits of globalization, and some actually suffer net losses'.

The North is in control not only due to strength but also because of lack of co-ordination in the South. National technology policies are largely determined by the work of global institutions and their rules and standards. It is vital that developing countries participate more forcefully and effectively in these institutions. This requires policy co-ordination among developing countries: 'Without policy co-ordination, Southern countries will stand to lose out in the formulation of international policy frameworks that will have important impact on their national policies'.

UNESCO's Communication Strategies

UNESCO's constitution requires the Organization to facilitate universal access to information through international co-operation, 'for the purpose of advancing .

the objectives of international peace and of the common welfare of mankind'. UNESCO pursues this mission by defending freedom of expression and its corollary freedom of the press, encouraging the development of pluralistic and independent media, promoting the free flow of information, ensuring that the new electronic media are of benefit to the greatest possible number of people and taking measures to avert the risks of uniformization and exclusion.

At the end of the cold war, the General Conference of UNESCO adopted a new communication strategy which, inter alia, solemnly reaffirmed the principle of the 'free flow of information' and reiterated that freedom of expression must be exercised 'without any obstacle'. With this return to constitutional basics, UNESCO regained its moral authority in this area. UNESCO is playing a leading role within the United Nations system for the defence and promotion of freedom of expression and its corollary, press freedom, which, in the words of the General Conference, is an 'essential component of any democratic society'.

Together with the United Nations, UNESCO organized five regional seminars on the promotion of independent and pluralistic media. Their conclusions and recommendations contained in the Declarations of Windhoek, Almaty, Santiago, Sana'a and Sofia were endorsed by the General Conference, as was the decision by the United Nations General Assembly taken at the initiative of UNESCO, to proclaim 3 May, the anniversary of the adoption of the Windhoek Declaration, 'World Press Freedom Day'. These activities and events have done much to promote freedom of expression worldwide. The launching in 1997 of the 'UNESCO-Guillermo Cano

World Press Freedom Prize', the Director-General's systematic public condemnation of crimes committed against journalists, and UNESCO's discreet diplomatic action on behalf of journalists and other intellectuals in prison or missing, are all examples of initiatives in keeping with this fundamental role of the Organization.

In several conflict zones, UNESCO is playing a pioneering role by helping to promote a culture of peace with and by the media. For more than five years now, in the countries of former Yugoslavia, the Organization has been offering assistance to independent media in order to preserve their freedom of expression. UNESCO has taken a number of initiatives to provide opportunities for exchange and co-operation among media professionals belonging to antagonistic national, ethnic or religious groups. This allows them to analyze together their attitudes towards each other and to create, through dialogue, a climate of mutual understanding to ease tension and foster reconciliation. The establishment of press houses in Rwanda and Burundi, open to both Tutsi and Hutu journalists, the setting up in Latin America of the REDIPAZ network and the launching in Jerusalem of the Israeli-Palestinian Media Forum, are examples of UNESCO's contribution to a culture of peace with and by the media.

UNESCO also makes a special effort to strengthen communication and information capacities in developing countries so that they can participate more actively in the communication process. This is done through the programmes and projects responding to the needs of these countries and of society in general. There is no doubt about the growing impact of communication media in today's society, both the conventional media (press, radio and television) and the information technologies such as the Internet, and the rapidly developing digital media. In this context, UNESCO has become a principal world forum for the discussion on such issues as Public Service Broadcasting and Editorial Independence; strengthening democratic voices; The Young and the Media - Tomorrow; and Sexual Abuse of Children, Child Pornography and Paedophilia on the Internet.

The Organization also issued a Global Study on Media Violence, based on a survey administered by leaders of the World Movement of Scout Organizations and computer-analyzed by Utrecht University. The UNESCO International Clearing House on Children and Violence on the Screen, established in February 1997 at the University of Gothenburg, regularly issues information on this subject, and published a yearbook entitled Children and Media Violence in 1998 and 1999.

Women and the media have also figured prominently in UNESCO's programme. Thousands of women media practitioners, people's movements, news and features services and information resources on women's issues participate in the WOMMED world network. A practical handbook, Women on the Net, has been issued in English and French and under a special project, Women Speaking to Women, community radio stations are run by women in six countries in Africa and Asia.

UNESCO's regional and national training programmes are an important part of communication development, particularly for independent local newspapers and community media. This work is further reinforced through the Global Network of Journalism Training Centres and Institutes organized in 1997 and launched with support from the International Programme for the Development of Communication (IPDC) in 1999. This complements the work done in universities by the UNESCO Chairs in Communication, including the most recent one created for communication technology for women at the Sook Myung University, Seoul.

International Programme for the Development of Communication

Freedom of expression is meaningful only when there is a wide range of media in existence, such as newspapers, radio stations and television channels. That is the basic philosophy on which the IPDC was founded. Established by a resolution of UNESCO's General Conference, it is a specialized programme focusing exclusively on building up the means of mass communication in developing countries. Since its establishment in 1980, IPDC has mobilized some $41 million in voluntary contributions for its special account and nearly $45 million for projects financed under funds-in-trust. Fellowships sponsored by individual countries have provided retraining for 1,500 communication professionals.

The projects carried out with IPDC funding cover a wide range of activities which seek to promote the concept of media pluralism and independence. They include the launching of community radio networks, newspapers for women and rural communities, the training of journalists for all types of media and the computerization of the editorial offices of news agencies, television channels, radio stations and newspapers. In addition, IPDC finances and supports the setting up of networks to denounce violations of press freedom.

In the area of information and informatics, UNESCO is promoting international development of both 'content' and 'infostructure'. UNESCO is fostering access to diversified content in cyberspace by promoting the concept of the electronic 'public domain', accessible on-line and off-line. The 'Publica' CD-ROM series of electronic documentary heritage, produced in co-operation with institutions in developing and developed countries and made available free of charge, covers, for example, electronic anthologies of development literature, free software and classical literature. The Memory of the World programme helps to inventory, preserve and disseminate the worlds documentary heritage including manuscripts of unique cultural significance.

UNESCO itself aims at providing a portal to the global 'cyber commons' of public domain information and applications through its own Web site, and regularly organizes activities to promote creativity and diversity on the Internet, such as through the annual UNESCO Web Prize awarded for outstanding achievements in creating Web sites in the areas of education, science, culture, and communication.

Another content-related focus concerns the use of electronic information to improve governance and facilitate democratization, which was the subject of a global UNESCO survey in 1998/99 to identify promising technologies, applications and approaches in this area of particular relevance for developing countries. Within its Infoyouth programme, UNESCO supports the establishment of Info-centres, info-skills and info-bulletins for young people.

In the 'infostructure' area, UNESCO provides assistance in the establishment of regional computer communication networks for public service applications and for new approaches to virtual communities for learning, for scientific exchange and for cultural development. Examples are a pilot project for the use of the Internet in priority development sectors in the Eastern Caribbean, extending the European Union's Trans-European Tele-Education Network (TEN) to four East European countries, the HeritageNet project linking libraries, archives, museums, art galleries and universities in Central Asia, and, in Africa, 'Learning Networks' enabling teachers to use the Internet for the improvement of education and multi-purpose community telecentres in rural or disadvantaged locations.

Since its beginnings, UNESCO has been promoting library and archive development through the preparation of guidelines and methodologies, advisory services, training of specialists and technical support to selected institutions. More recently, over 300 libraries have been linked through the UNESCO Network of Associated Libraries (UNAL) which was launched in 1990, and within the MEDLIB project major libraries in the Mediterranean region are focusing together on improving the management of and access to electronic information.

Given the critical importance of skills for the development of an information society, UNESCO pays particular attention to the training of information professionals (librarians, archivists, documentalists, computer specialists), as well as of users at all levels. For example, a complete modular framework for training in informatics, covering undergraduate, and postgraduate and continuing education programmes, has been developed in collaboration with the International Federation for Information Processing (IFIP) to serve as a framework for development, testing and international exchange of training materials in these areas.

Sustainability

An important concern has arisen in connection with the possible proliferation of digital technologies in the developing countries, namely, whether ICTs can be used in environmentally sustainable ways. The global use of ICTs would drastically increase the emission of carbon dioxide (from printers, copiers, computers, and so on) to environmentally untenable levels. More ICTs would also imply more production of computers. The production of a single PC requires approximately as much energy as the average electricity consumption of a European household per year. One PC needs twenty tons of natural resources and after three to four years when the equipment is obsolete, the PC will be dumped on the growing heap of electronic scrap, along with toxic waste such as cadmium (in the batteries) and lead (in the screens). The situation has to be seen in the light of a rapidly growing world population which could by the mid-21st century amount to some 12,000 million people.

Knowledge

One essential dimension of human development is knowledge, crucial in enabling people to broaden their choices. ICTs are the basic tools of emerging knowledge-based societies. They represent an important shift from the utilization of natural and material resources to the deployment of data and information and related analytical and processing skills. This development is, however, accompanied by national information and informatics policies through guidelines, workshops and technical assistance. Special consideration is given to 'info-ethical' questions, to achieving a balance between the common good and economic imperatives, and to facilitating the use of information and communication technologies for development purposes by the public sector and the civil society.

A strong commitment by the international community is necessary to ensure that commercial interest do not dominate the development of ICTs in the world, more particularly in developing countries. Governments, public and private institutions have to assume their responsibilities if the gap between information-rich and information-poor is not to continue to widen a strong trend toward the privatization and commercialization of knowledge sources and the concurrent enforcement of legal measures to protect private intellectual property. The emerging global regime for Intellectual Property Rights (IPR) tends to give more emphasis to the economic aspects of IPR protection than to public interest considerations. There is a dominant economic angle in this regime which gives priority to the interests of large producers over those of small creators and consumers.

The central focus is on the misappropriation of corporate property rather than on artistic and literary creativity. The move to give IPR protection to material in the public domain when it has been entered in an electronic database could render access to knowledge more costly - and thus prohibitive - for large numbers of people. In addition, the initiative to extend copyright protection to all forms of digital copying could make the Internet a pay-per-view medium creating obstacles to the access to knowledge for those who cannot pay. Developments in the international regime for intellectual property protection are an attempt to create and maintain a balance between a set of rival claims to the control over knowledge and its dissemination.

The protection of intellectual property rights must provide the incentives, rewards and recognition for individual producers of knowledge in order to stimulate progress. Benefits for the creator, and public access to artistic, literary and scientific works must both be secured. Whereas IPR protection seeks to promote the progress of science, it also restricts access to knowledge, since it defines knowledge as private property and has a tendency to facilitate monopolistic tendencies.

It may well be that the current trends in the trade-oriented IPR regime lead to more restricted access rather than better public distribution. Although an absence of legal protection could have adverse effects on intellectual production, the move toward overprotection is 'not conducive to access to the networks by research workers and academics of developing countries'.

ICT developments are more technology driven than user oriented. If the ICT potential for human development is to be successfully exploited, the needs and aspirations of users must be central to the whole process of design, construction and application. Present experience is concisely summed up by Mansell and Wehn:

> 'There is substantial evidence that if applications do not reflect user needs or involve them in the process of development, they simply will not bring the expected benefits. They are likely to create new problems that will be costly to address. If the specific

> social, cultural, and economic conditions, the expertise and commitment of users, and components of the infrastructure are not assembled together, ICT applications will fail to yield benefits'.

The essential requirement of user orientation is hampered by the strong tendency to delegate social responsibility for the governance of the ICT-sector to a global trade regime. In fact, the politics of world communication represent a historical shift from a public service orientation to private competition with a predominantly commercial focus.

ICTs and Cultural Production

The information and communication technologies (ICTs) are advancing with unprecedented speed, particularly in the most economically developed countries, it would be a mistake to regard them as solely responsible for the current changes. This long-heralded momentum, which seemed slow at the beginning but is now well under way, seems likely to continue at a rapid pace and, if some authors are to be believed, will usher in a new information society or information age. It is, however, one thing to note the dynamic development of telecommunications, information technology and the audiovisual media, and quite another to credit them with changes in culture and in other areas of social life.

Technical innovation is a by-product - only rarely a driving force - of transformations whose origin lies elsewhere. Technology provides such changes with new areas of opportunity, encouraging activities which would otherwise have been blocked by the dominant organizations in the sector and weakening the barriers set up to defend vested interests or to safeguard specific practices. It is important to look beyond the usual thought patterns, which see the issue as one of adaptation to technological changes, and turn our attention instead to changing trends in cultural production.

ICTs may strengthen cultural production and help it to gain widespread recognition, or conversely, they may cause it to be confined to a restricted area or even to decline. Throughout the world, cultural production tends to be community based. Anthropologists, historians and cultural sociologists rightly emphasize this recurring feature which explains the persistence of locally-rooted and even non-commercial forms of culture, as well as the different ways in which viewers interpret television series, according to their own culture. In other words, despite more than two centuries of industrialized cultural production and despite the aggressive strategies of the increasingly-powerful communications groups, independent forms of entertainment still thrive all over the world. Folk productions are not declining - far from it: books and newspapers are published, films and television series are produced and music is recorded independently of the major companies.

The pessimistic forecasts of the imminent globalization of cultural production heard over the last two decades have been proved wrong - or at least exaggerated. Culture remains an area of social activity in which industrialization meets with resistance and constraints, even though increasingly governed by markets, and despite a growing trend towards the internationalization of production and the transnationalization of subjects, styles and standards. The fact that predictions have not so far been fulfilled is, however, no guarantee for the future.

ICTs and the momentum they undoubtedly generate will eventually provide the means to move decisively ahead towards the industrialization and internationalization of cultural production. What in the past was only partly successful is now allegedly resulting directly from ICTs. In other words, what the mass audiovisual media merely launched in the past has now become firmly established and universal through ICTs, which have proven to be more successful at sidestepping the cultural structures of countries and peoples, and certainly more favourable to the worldwide circulation of transnational flows. Individual tools of communi-cation and/or access to data and ready-made programmes are ushering in sweeping transformations in cultural production.

The history of the cultural industries is by no means linear. Until recently, it has progressed unevenly, whenever production techniques were adopted and made widely available, so that works of literature became accessible as books, musical works as records, and films and audiovisual works as screenings in cinemas or as video cassettes. The industrialization of culture has, however, encountered difficulties and setbacks. For producers and publishers, the values attached to culture usually act as 'restrictions', or at any rate as contingencies, for which marketing techniques have yet to be found.

It has been more convenient to market the equipment used to deliver cultural works than to introduce successfully on to the market works available either in a physical medium or accessible through projection or broadcasting by the audiovisual media. So the picture of the relationship between culture and industry today presents sharp contrasts.

There are striking divergences between:

— developed and developing countries;

— countries which give more or less free rein to market forces, and those in which the public authorities provide impetus and co-ordination;

— countries where the market and industry are the major controlling factors in the cultural sphere, and those where small-scale productions, live entertainment with a popular appeal and non-commercial productions predominate;

— the various art forms: it is very difficult to create added value in dance, poetry and narrative performances, as opposed to filmed enter-tainment, which should be considered an activity straddling art and industry;

— individual access to works and live entertainment;

— cultural productions broadcast through the mass audiovisual media and those which, once published, are bought by consumers.

Nevertheless, ICTs are capable of strongly reinforcing trends begun at least two decades ago, thereby giving a decisive boost to the expansion of cultural industries. The areas in which ICTs can make an impact need to be carefully evaluated, however. Contrary to what professionals often claim, it would be wrong to expect multimedia production to create innovative products - apart from games -and important markets in the short term. Innovative products of a truly multimedia type are still too rare and production costs remain too high for rapid progress to be expected.

If there is not a rapid change in product design and production methods during the next decade, ICTs will probably not be instrumental in extending the scope of commercial and even industrialized culture, since with the products which are currently available they are increasingly marginalizing certain cultures, standardizing universally accessible products and excluding those who lack the purchasing power to be ICT consumers. The solution to this problem would appear relatively easy and involves speeding up product flow, which is the second major feature of the development of the cultural industries.

Distance-shopping for products hitherto almost e xclusively supplied by specialized end-product distributors or by mass distribution outlets, and downloading products accessible from a distance are two activities that have been made possible by the efficiency of communications networks and the growing sophistication of access terminals. The scope of this new electronic commerce is still difficult to gauge, but there is no doubt that in 1997-98 its growth was such that the major distribution groups all rushed headlong in that direction, preceded by small pioneering firms. This strategic choice was made despite the fact that monetary transactions on the Internet are still not totally safe and that arrangements for remunerating artists and publishers are still under negotiation.

Most specialists consider that cultural products are particularly well-suited to this new form of distribution. There are substantial advantages for consumers: real-time access; the opportunity to browse through all available catalogues and products; access to catalogues of foreign firms which used to be accessible only, if at all, with long delays involved. In other words, these new ways of accessing cultural products are of special interest both to the consumers least concerned by mass products, and to specialist publishers and producers.

Paradoxically, the people who are apparently the most critical of this rapid change in the distribution of cultural products ('cultivated' members of society, let us say, who prefer the existing methods of accessing art forms, and also scientists) are those who, for the moment, find it most advantageous to purchase directly via the networks.

There is an additional paradoxical aspect to these immediate advantages for the most selective and demanding users. Producers and artists who offer the most distinctive products and who frequently encounter great difficulty in distributing the works they create and publish will obviously be tempted to bypass the large broadcasters and distributors (who demand a high percentage of the selling price) in order to contact consumers directly. This is all the more likely to happen because, throughout the history of the cultural industries, artists and their publishers have tried to eliminate intermediaries with little success. They themselves then joined that enviable group, thus only reinforcing the existing oligopolies.

The current trend consists mainly of users purchasing products after browsing through catalogues on publishers' sites and on the sites of artists acting as producers of their own works. Soon it will be possible to download actual works, meaning that publishers of books and recorded music will no longer need to reproduce and record the work in a physical medium. This is not a utopian prospect; it is already possible to access literary and musical works in this way, or even extracts from them. This phenomenon raises two essential questions about cultural products. Is a work on offer a finished product just because it has been stabilized in a medium? Next, have the forms of monetary payment by consumers, here encouraged to buy works piecemeal, and 'paying-as-they-go', been fully considered? These are not merely technical innovations which, by encouraging a commercial shift, coincide with changes in systems of accessing works. Here technical innovations are changing the very substance of cultural products in various ways, especially by calling into question their finished appearance, an aspect considered fundamental up until now.

In modern societies, the values and images associated with the concepts of leisure, information and culture are still sharply differentiated. Although these concepts are evolving and now sometimes overlap, it would nonetheless hardly be possible to confuse them taken in a strict sense. They have relatively stable definitions: infor-mation is more ephemeral than culture, and this idea orients the functioning of those who produce news and information; leisure time is primarily for entertainment, but leisure pursuits encouraging the development of cultural activities are judged as positive. Although the trend began earlier, ICTs are causing these distinctions to grow more and more blurred, and in some cases it is becoming difficult to distinguish between information products and cultural products.

Methods of creation (by journalists or artists, with an increasing use of streamlined methods), production structures (more and more often controlled by the same multimedia groups), distribution procedures (via networks or in the form of products accessible on- or off-line), consumption time and conditions of consumer use (use is often individual and involves interactivity with the hardware acting as intermediary in programme communication) are now closely related, not to say identical. These similarities cannot be considered as either secondary or insignificant.

Behind all the confusions and convergences, the question that arises is more than ever that of mass culture, although in forms different from those observed in the 1960s when the phenomenon became evident. As the transmission of standardized and increasingly transnational mass culture boosted by ICTs develops, cultural distinc-tiveness tends to be maintained within an elitist, or at any rate a niche, context.

Although distinctive cultural production is not declining, and examples of it which successfully express popular and national identities continue to receive considerable attention, they enter into competition with mass products that are easily distributed on communication networks. The struggle is to some extent unequal, not because of inadequacy of supply but because the major communications groups are strengthening their hold on the circulation of products. Insofar as future developments can be inferred from the situation today, culture seems to be going the same way as leisure and information. For most people, ICTs have not yet become part of a familiar landscape. They have already led, however, to some fairly radical changes in the functioning and regulation of public services, resulting in considerable hesitation on the part of those responsible for cultural policy.

An increase in the supply of commercial products almost inevitably leads to the reduction, if not the disappearance, of non-commercial products (heavily subsidized by public funds) and of semi-commercial products (e.g. small-scale productions and those enjoying tax and customs protection). A movement of this type has recently become apparent in television production. In response to competition from powerful new commercial channels and in order to increase their output of programmes to compete with the commercial channels, with approximately the same resources, the managers of public channels have been obliged to subcontract production, placing it in the hands of new private producers for whom the origin of the orders they handle is of no importance.

As a result, production variety in public television programmes has declined sharply, and some types of programme are less available or have actually disappeared since they are not commercially viable in a situation where audience ratings are all-important. Poetry and other literary programmes have disap-peared or been banished from prime-time slots. Even once-popular variety shows have been downsized or incorporated into shows with a wider appeal, since the popularity of a group or singer is no longer sufficient in itself to attract a mass audience. Over the past ten or fifteen years, some national cultural industries have continued to function and have even grown as a result of certain trends in public policy.

In the European Union, community-wide or domestic measures have undoubtedly been beneficial to certain industries in Member States, such as book publishing (the French system of retail price maintenance for books has allowed a network of specialized bookshops to survive), recorded music publishing (radio stations are obliged to play a quota of nationally-produced songs and music), cinema and audiovisual production (a system incorporating various forms of aid to production) and television production.

There is, however, no guarantee that these hitherto undeniably advantageous effects will continue in the future. Not only do quota systems run into operational difficulties attracting regular criticism because of their singularity in world commercial transactions, but the fact that programmes can now circulate on the networks and largely escape control from public authorities will tend to reduce the effectiveness of support measures for small- and medium-sized industries operating mainly within a specific cultural or linguistic framework. This does not mean that such measures are unnecessary, but that their effectiveness may become more uncertain, simply because con-sumers will tend to diversify demand, including demand for products from the sphere of high culture.

A number of authors representing different schools of thought have long been predicting a trend towards the individualization of social behaviour, and the emergence of this trend does seem to be reinforced by ICTs, particularly in the developed countries. ICTs, unlike the media that developed earlier, usually require user-consumers to take active steps not only to access a specific programme but also to interact with it in order to obtain responses tailored to their personal requirements. To this extent, ICTs, more than any other earlier technology, promote a one-to-one correspondence between the content on offer and the user's demands, which are apparently unlike those of anyone else.

Where ICTs are involved, cultural consumption is not simply a question of narcissistic contact with works. Likewise, collective forms of consumption are not doomed to disappear, because individualization does not necessarily spell a decline in public performances and other forms of collective entertainment. Despite predictions to the contrary, the proliferation of individual delivery systems for recorded music has not led to a decline in concerts of all types of music. Complex interactions and processes of mutual i n fluence are observably taking place between different types of music, but it is not to be expected that this will have any practical outcome, although new linkages can be foreseen.

ICTs encourage a fragmented, episodic pace of consumption which has little in common with the heyday of collective cultural consumption and this tendency may lead to a number of fundamental cultural changes. One consequence may be for increased cultural consumption to go hand in hand with a decline in discussion and debate focused on cultural productions. It is also possible that performances may become almost exclusively opportunities for the 'promotion' of cultural merchandise, something that would be inevitable if public aid earmarked for live performances were reduced or even abolished, with those responsible taking as their pretext the variety and quantity of commercial products available. This would mark the culmination of the process by which culture becomes a commercial product and, as noted above, is absorbed into the leisure and information sectors.

ICTs have promted American English to the status of an international language. According to a 1998 Euromarketing study, more than one of every two

Internet surfers (58%) uses English. Other languages - Spanish (8.7%), German (8.6%), Japanese (7.9%) and French (3.7%) - are much less commonly used. These data, which are obviously difficult to establish, have nevertheless been confirmed by other studies. However, they are difficult to assess because change is so rapid in both hardware and habits.

Furthermore, it is not possible, on the basis of data on the preferred language of communication (used for electronic mail and forums), to draw similar conclusions regarding trade in cultural products. For example, after an initial phase when English.. predominated, the satellite channels are now beginning to diversify into other languages. Will automatic translation systems contain applications that will help to reduce misunderstandings between languages and promote genuine multilingualism?

In the past, research has proved disappointing, and researchers are at present cautious, pinning their hopes on the development of computer-assisted translation systems. This indicates recognition of the fact that, in this field, approximations and simplifications are not sufficient, because they undermine languages as vehicles of specific cultural features. Only strong support for translation from producers and from authorities responsible for public policy can help to bring about a more balanced flow of cultural works. If this is not forthcoming, English and probably a few more of the most widely spoken languages will eventually dominate the cultural marketplace.

Support for translation and for the development of translation aid systems will not, however, be enough in the absence of systematic efforts to support productions suitable for distribution outside their country or region of origin, and support in distributing them. Recent experience has shown that the successful exportation of films, works for television and sound broadcasting or even literary works, depends as much on international standards being met as on the availability of an appropriate distribution system. It is also important for production costs on national broadcasting networks to have been absorbed in advance, which explains the recent success of Brazilian and Mexican series outside the areas where they were produced. The same factors are likely to be important in the future.

Although in theory the new communications networks guarantee wider distribution, and even distribution that crosses borders and cuts out intermediaries, which may be helpful for niche products that may even be boycotted in their place of origin, it would be illusory to think that world markets will develop on this basis. Direct transactions will leave room for a few new actors, but free flow will probably lead to a rapid jump in production costs and a concentration of distributors. The major communi-cation groups are preparing for this eventuality. Their uncertainties about the future focus on the plans of their direct competitors rather than on the emergence of newcomers or the development of direct commerce that would be beyond their control.

ICTs undeniably complicate a number of issues facing the production of culture in all its diversity. However, the more or less rapid spread of hardware and networks is not the only factor involved in sustaining artistic pluralism within countries and regions and keeping a variety of production methods in place. Blithe and often exaggerated statements to the effect that we are now living in an information society which will impose its ground rules on culture should be viewed sceptically. It should also be remembered that, for complex reasons that research into technical innovation has already begun to elucidate, technical developments seldom fulfil expert predictions. In other words, ICTs do not contain a blueprint for the future. They will not be the sole factors shaping the future. If, however, those responsible for cultural production worldwide adopt a wait-and-see attitude and fail to grasp the importance of what is at stake, then culture will be increasingly subservient to the norms of mediatized communication and information flows.

In conclusion, it must be emphasized that public cultural policies are important and should be reinstated in areas where the field has been left free for the commercial audiovisual media and transborder flows of information. Public action will have little effect, however, if it is confined to protective and defensive measures which are in any case liable to be inefficient, if not impossible, to implement. This issue is likely to give rise to considerable debate and to social movements and even 'resistance' instigated by artists, producers, users and political leaders. During the 1993 General Agreement on Tariffs and Trade (GATT) negotiations, France strongly supported the idea of 'making an exception of culture' and provisionally won its case, arguing that with the opening of world markets, cultural products should not be treated like other commercial commodities.

Since then, the question has been asked worldwide, some counting on a de facto abolition of the 'cultural exception' by technological development, while others are waiting for international organizations and regional bodies to come out in support of cultural pluralism.

Another crucial issue being debated is the future of copyright and authors' continuing control over their works in an environment complicated by the emergence of multimedia products. Many developing countries have not yet stated that they are directly concerned by these discussions, which nevertheless do affect them.

In order to maintain cultural pluralism, it is pointless to avoid or side-step negotiations on these basic issues. An attempt was made to do this in the case of the Multilateral Agreement on Investment (MAI) by seeking to negotiate behind closed doors within the OECD. What are needed are balanced agreements that acknowledge the distinctive nature of cultural products and do not treat them simply as industrial goods.

Impact on the Media

The increasingly interconnected nature of the mass media industry has encouraged integration in a complex variety of reciprocal connections. The first set of logical mergers were between different types of media, such as television with radio and the press to create multimedia conglomerates. Mergers of media entities across countries and regions also occurred in order to attain the critical business strength needed to reach global markets.

A few hardware manufacturers made strategic moves to purchase media houses producing films, music and other media products. The strategy has paid off in recent years through co-ordinated releases of new generations of hardware, such as Digital Versatile Disk (DVD) players, digital television receivers, and digital music recording devices, together with media products and software to be played back on these new devices.

The synergy is mutually beneficial. There would have been no demand for the hardware had there been a lack of attractive media products to play on the devices.

Without the devices, the media companies would not have been able to launch a new generation of both old and new releases which help to produce a new stream of revenue for the existing libraries of intellectual properties owned by these media companies. In an interesting new twist to integration and convergence, a major television sports broadcaster has mounted a takeover of one of the most famous soccer teams in the world.

The business strategy is to acquire full control of broadcast and merchandising rights through the outright purchase of the team. If this proves to be a profitable move, it is not impossible that media companies may begin to purchase properties as diverse as universities and restaurants in order to secure publication copyright for scholarly titles and courses, and broadcast licences for cookery programmes.

There are two sides to integration and convergence. The case against concentration of ownership can be seen within the printing sector in the United States, where extensive research shows that the twelve largest newspaper conglomerates control almost 50% of all circulation in the largest market for news in the world. In book publishing, nearly every one of the major commercial publishing companies has also been bought and assimilated into larger businesses, while independent bookstores are being forced out of business by a handful of powerful national chains. On the positive side, the sale of some cable television companies, again in the United tates, helped raise much-needed financial investment to upgrade distribution systems. The merger of Cable News Network (CNN) with the Time Warner group led to the pooling of extensive complementary intellectual properties, particularly in politics, which has resulted in service on the Internet which offers more depth and data than either company alone could have provided in the print and television media.

The expansionary trends of the media conglomerates, coupled with media technologies which ignore political borders, have forced government-owned media organizations in newly developed and developing countries to respond. Within Asia, the response has generally been to privatize state-owned media in an effort to make them more competitive and attractive to domestic audiences. However, the privatization has been structured in such a way as to protect, preserve and empower traditional cultural values and maintain key government controls at the same time. The Association of South-East Asian Nations (ASEAN) plans to launch a regional direct satellite television broadcast channel, but these plans have been delayed by the financial problems affecting the region.

When several large media organizations merge, they create media giants with huge audiences. This is an invaluable asset which helps in maximizing advertising revenue, the lifeblood of media. The merger also pools strategic market information, such as subscriber and advertiser databases which are used to cross-sell media products and advertising across the organizations within the merged group.

Direct selling is probably the showcase innovation of the private sector on the Internet, and Amazon.com is the current undisputed star in this area. Amazon began by selling books over its Internet site and subsequently added music CDs to its virtual bookstore. A strictly e-commerce company, it has captured the imagination of media organizations because it has so far dealt exclusively with media products. Indications are that it will diversify rapidly to include a large variety of consumer products.

Every media company with tangible products must at some time have reviewed Amazon's methods for possible emulation. The arithmetic of direct selling to consumers worldwide without having to incur high distribution and sales discounts is an irresistible idea, and an increasing number of media organizations with such product offerings have launched websites to test the feasibility of an Amazon-like sales outlet. Attracting less public attention, but perhaps more exciting in its technological concept, are the direct sales facilities of newspapers, journals, bulletins, and electronic book publishers. Amazon uses the Internet only to promote and process payment for a product before resorting to fairly conventional means for delivering a traditional tangible media product to the consumer. In contrast to this, specialized publishers are offering articles and information from databases for instantaneous downloading over the Internet immediately after a payment has been made at the site. Book publishers will be interested in the mass consumer response to several electronic book devices introduced recently into the market and which approximate the size and feel of a book. They lend themselves to the direct sales of books bought and delivered over e-commerce systems.

The North American book distributor Barnes & Noble has negotiated with various publishers to offer more than 1,000 titles of books for downloading into the devices which have a capacity to store anything from about 1,000 to 500,000 pages at any one time. The e-book is an extremely attractive proposition to book publishers because they do not have to commit expensive print-runs and warehousing expenses up front; the risks are therefore minimum. This may encourage publishers to accept a larger number of manuscripts for publication. It is likely to facilitate the release of traditionally short-run titles, which have been rejected in the past because they were not viable as expensive paper editions.

The e-book is a viable alternative to currently available publish-on-demand technology, which deploys high-speed photocopying machines linked to collating and binding machinery. The music industry may be on the verge of making similar direct sales. A new device which downloads and stores audio digital recordings from the Internet for repeated playback by consumers was cleared for public sale, following a court hearing in California (USA) to determine if such a device threatened the preservation of intellectual property rights. The legal endorsement for the device has set the stage for music to be sold directly to consumers, a song or 'cut' at a time, rather than as a compilation on longer-playing discs.

New Business Models

The evolution of a new generation of media technologies has presented the industry with many possibilities for developing new products and services. One of the key factors, which will help in identifying the final list of possibilities for sustained development, is the parallel evolution of business models applicable to these possibilities. The successful candidates must operate with a business model acceptable to the consumers, and attractive enough to engage media operators.

The private sector has long been the primary source for funding of media operations in North America, Europe, Latin America and parts of Asia. With the trend towards the privatization of state-owned media in developing countries, the importance of feasible business models has become critical in the determination of how technologies will be deployed, and what content and software will be offered.

Large audience base models

This type of business model dominate for traditional mass media such as radio, print and television. It has also become one of the most important models for Internet-related operations where 'portal' sites offering search and directory services to the vast World Wide Web have drawn the largest number of users and attracted the keenest interest of investors and entrepreneurs. As with most broadcast organizations, portal sites do not charge for their services but instead derive revenues by selling advertising.

In this model, the number of people served by a particular Web site or broadcasting station is crucial in determining the pricing of its advertisements, and eventually its revenue. The same applies to the print media products, which are often priced for the recovery of production and distribution costs only, while profits and creative costs derive from the sale of advertising space. These numbers will take on added importance when members of the audience become customers and shoppers on interactive television and electronic commerce Web sites.

New audience-tracking technologies and sophisticated audience research methodologies enable these numbers to be desegregated into groups with a high propensity to purchase certain goods and services. These advances are a boon to advertisers and will pose a challenge to media operators, who, in the past, were required simply to broadcast advertisements for large groups. The tougher requirements are already apparent in advertising at Web sites where operators are required to broadcast advertisements in the style of banners at the top or bottom of specified Web pages, and the cost of advertising was determined by the number of people accessing the page and seeing the advertisements. This simple formula became a little more complicated when the cost was computed on the basis of the number of people who clicked on the banners and visited the Web site linked to the advertisements. The third formula which is evolving will very likely be based on a sales commission on the actual business transacted as a result of exposure, click-throughs and other services rendered at a particular Web site or page.

Electronic commerce model

This model has captured the imagination of the industry as the most appropriate for the Internet with Amazon.com as the premier prototype company. Amazon has demonstrated both the potential and the problems of this model. Although it is popularly cited as the most successful electronic commerce company, it has not shown a profit since it started. On the contrary, Amazon consistently incurred losses until the end of 1998. Researchers who have tracked the company's exponential growth blame the losses on high operating costs. Its economics also reveal a staggering scale of business. One study estimated that Amazon must generate $1 billion in annual sales just to break even.

The electronic publishing model has been given a boost with the introduction of secure electronic transaction software and systems which permit payments for purchases made over the Internet to be securely debited from credit card accounts. Further progress is expected in the near future when 'smart cards', which enable payment purchases using secure computer codes, are launched worldwide.

Subscription access model

Subscription access was widely thought to be a promising model for the electronic publishing of newspapers, magazines, journals, and newsletters. The typical electronic subscription begins when a person makes a lump sum payment to the publisher, who then provides the subscriber with a unique password, which then permits access to each new edition at a Web site.

Although the model was based on very sound logic, it was not well received by people on the Internet. For the present, it appears that the founding principle of the Internet for the free sharing of information still persists. Major content providers have indefinitely postponed plans to charge for access to their sites. To replace this, some providers require visitors to their Web sites to register themselves, or encourage them to click on the advertisement of a corporate sponsor, as a kind of surrogate payment. This has caused extensive revisions in the business plans of media companies started for the exclusive purpose of publishing and selling information over the Internet.

Conventional media, such as television news networks, newspapers, and magazines, which extended their dissemination by recycling selections from their products on the Internet, have enjoyed more prosperity. Their sites regularly clock up millions of visitors each month who in turn each read several Web pages and help to generate a total of many millions more 'page views' for the sites.

While people visiting the sites do not pay for their visits, the media organizations running the sites benefit in several ways: firstly, by promoting or cross-selling their flagship on printed or broadcast products via free access to excerpts at the Web site; secondly, by offering archival information such as previously published articles or transcripts of old broadcasts for sale through an automated system of database searches and electronic commerce; and lastly, by exposing people to this new outlet for their products and developing a global audience for future sales of a new generation of products and services.

The Economist and The Wall Street Journal now publish simultaneously on paper and on the Internet. There are many sites on the Internet that provide news. One type are the special Internet news sites, often provided by the Internet Service Providers (ISPs). Others are sites maintained by already-existing newspapers as a complement to the printed product. One can find daily newspapers and news-oriented periodicals from almost every country in the world, representing a mixture of national and regional/local press, as well as news targeting specific groups in terms of language and/or ethnic belonging. One significant result of this development is that, whereas the possibilities of access to traditionally disseminated press were limited, especially concerning regional and local press, news via the Internet means worldwide dissemination.

The former provides subscribers to the printed product and free access to the Internet edition. The latter sells subscription access to both versions. Some newspapers have used their Internet editions to enhance the attractiveness of their classified advertisements by offering package deals, which place such advertisements simultaneously on both printed and Internet editions.

As a result of the financial crisis of 1997/98, media organizations throughout Asia, Latin America and Russia are struggling to stay solvent. The media in these regions have been hit by high increases in repayments of bank loans and other forms of business financing, increases in the price of newsprint, and significant drops in advertising revenue, as companies have trimmed their advertising budgets as part of cost-cutting measures.

Internet services providers have suffered from the crisis as well, because the values of local currencies have fallen in relation to the US dollar in which the cost of telecommunications connections are calculated. At the same time and for the same reason, the cost of imported networking hardware and soft-ware has also increased. Many media companies will therefore consider the new technologies with an eye on costs and their potential contribution to cost cutting.

Communication Development

The tendency to use new technologies to meet commercial objectives is problematic for people and regions without the necessary financial resources to attract companies to fulfil their needs. The challenge is made harder by the need for stable telecommunication links and electricity to power nearly all the new technologies. Both are in short supply in the poorest regions.

The case of developing countries illustrates the way in which technology evolves and is diffused at different speeds across the world. Whereas new technologies are represented by state-of-the-art digital innovations in the developed world, for parts of the developing world telephones, television or even radio may be the latest technologies. It is in this context that two recent innovations in radio broadcasting represent important advances in the medium. The clockwork (or wind-up) radio is the first.

Communication specialists in development have been aware of the problem faced by isolated communities in obtaining dry-cell batteries to power radio receivers for several decades. Crystal-sets and solar-powered receivers have not proved to be entirely successful. The clockwork radio is powered by a patented power source, which with a few minutes of winding-up will keep a receiver playing for about an hour. It is an exciting invention which has been adapted to work on lap-top computers and other devices, which previously depended on batteries for electrical power. For the present, the relatively high-costs of these radio sets prevent their extensive diffusion across the developing world.

The other innovation is at the broadcaster's end. UNESCO has taken the lead in helping to develop affordable low-power radio transmitters for operating community broadcasting services. These transmitters are assembled from generic components by local technicians, who also assist with maintenance. Such services facilite the decentralization of media control to the community. They help promote participatory communication, which empowers communities, and support the planning and implementation of sustainable development programmes. The main hindrance to the spread of this technology is legislative.

Most developing - and even developed - countries discourage community broadcasting by limiting access to radio frequencies and to a broadcasting licence. A classic example of a new technology converging to support an old predecessor is the technology to stream sound over the Internet. This is the developed world's version of the developing world's evolution towards community broadcasting. The technology is very affordable at both ends. People can receive such Internet radio broadcasts with a relatively low investment while broadcasters can be 'on the air' broadcasting literally to the whole world at very minimal cost. These technologies represent an extremely small fraction of the total number of innovations introduced into the media industry.

The developing world with its highly limited purchasing power has sustained minimal research and development efforts to increase their access to relevant content and channels of mass communication. A study in the Philippines found that where privatization of media has been the norm, programming is not meeting the needs of local populations. This sentiment may extend quite widely across the developing world.

Transmission frequencies are a very valuable resource in some areas of the world where finding a frequency for broadcasting to minority groups is a daunting uphill battle, since regulatory authorities and established media companies have vested interests to protect. The introduction of digital television broadcasting technology with the capacity to place four channels in the same space that one analogue channel used to occupy, will soon make plenty of new broadcasting space available. A significant amount of this newly freed-up space should be reserved for minority interest broadcasting, which is now limited.

Developing countries will probably have to wait for several years before the cost of digital technologies reaches an affordable level. The early users, namely the developed countries, should therefore establish a precedent for safeguarding minority interests and those of disadvantaged groups by reserving such open digital spaces for them. Spaces must be held in trust, not only for minorities, but also for the common good in areas such as education, science and culture, which are not very profitable, but are socially vital.

The ICT technologies, with their capacities to move multimedia content anywhere in the world in a matter of seconds, provide the perfect tool for gathering and disseminating news. They have become available at a time when the demand for news is rising rapidly, fuelled by the globalization of trade and national economies. The increasing demand is not only for a greater quantity of news, but also for higher speeds in reporting. This in turn presents developers of technology with demands to increase further the capabilities and speed of technologies creating a powerful iterative spiral, which will lead to even more, exciting technologies.

The demand for news worldwide is obviously not uniform. Television ratings are a good yardstick by which to gauge demand. News dominated the top ten television shows in the United States; soap operas of different origins seem to be the most popular in many other countries such as Brazil, China and South Africa. The demand for news over the Internet appears to be more consistent, with nearly all news sites registering the most number of visitors and Web pages downloaded. Sites operated by newspapers around the world commonly serve millions of page views per month.

While most newspapers continue to provide only text and static images on their Web sites, radio, television and other integrated media conglomerates now offer multimedia content which includes text, and sound and video clips of headline news items. Several financial publications operate Web sites with access to constantly updated databases and expert systems software to work out investment computations and projections.

The exponential growth of the Internet as a channel for distributing news can be seen in the meteoric growth of Microsoft National Broadcasting Company (MSNBC), a joint venture between Microsoft and the National Broadcasting Company (NBC) in the United States.

By the first quarter of 1998, the news site served an average of 300,000 users a day with the occasional peak of 900,000 users. Together, they read 200 million pages a month. Measured by reach, it is the fifth largest daily newspaper in the United States. The top four Internet news sites in the country, MSNBC, USA Today, CNN and the American Broadcasting Company, collectively serve up 700 million pages of news every month.

Direct satellite broadcast television news channels and the Internet benefit people around the world who want and need to have constantly updated access to news at all times of the day and night. This has caused an insatiable demand for the latest news, which has in turn created the twenty-four-hour news cycle. News operations in the past were governed by deadlines fixed by printing schedules, in the case of newspapers and magazines, and airtimes for conventional radio and television news. Now that the audience is global, every moment of the day and night is the deadline.

All news programming is by definition perpetually incomplete and in a state of being constantly updated. The concept of 'the edition' has been replaced by devices such as 'breaking news' when regular programming is interrupted in television broadcasts, to show raw, unedited, live coverage about a still-evolving news item. On the Internet, a similar device is the 'latest' button, which provides a link to a usually brief write-up of a news event in the making.

The race to be the first on the air or the Internet with the latest news has created an approach to news reporting which concentrates on the immediate, the gathering of eye-witness accounts, and a follow-up of the event as it unfurls and draws to a conclusion. Attention to analytical writing is on the decline. The twenty-four-hour news cycle, and the quickly changing news agenda discourages reflection, research and analysis which take up time, and time is what the editorial departments no longer have to spare. The result is sometimes news reporting which is disconnected from history and the broader geo-political context. Merrill Brown, editor-in-chief of MSNBC, is mindful of the shortcomings of journalism on the Internet: 'Those of us producing for the Internet haven't always been as thoughtful as we might about putting today's incremental developments into perspective'. Andrew Heyward, the News President of Columbia Broadcasting System (CBS), one of the dominant North American television networks, is equally conscious of television's short-falls. He identified 'the seven daily sins of television news' as imitation, predictability, artificiality, laziness, oversimplification, hype and cynicism.

Although not as profitable as the owners would like, the media is now big business. During the con-centration of ownership, large financial investments were made; owners are now eager to recover them. At the same time, profits at many media organizations have shrunk. Together, these considerations have driven media organizations to cut costs and this has harmed the quality and diversity of news services. Among the elements which have been slashed are foreign news bureaus and the amount of original reporting undertaken.

News editors are also less inclined to dispatch their own reporters, photographers and camera crews to cover an event, preferring instead to rewrite wire service stories and tap into news footages from large television news agencies. The impact of this trend is a significantly reduced plurality of perspectives, especially where international news items are concerned. The same television news clips are broadcast by stations around the world, while the same wire service dispatches are carried in the newspapers. This provides the handful of international news agencies which feed the media. organizations around the world with an oligarchic grip on the flow of news and views. This phenomenon is called 'consonance'. Research has shown that the further the geographic origin of a news story from the editorial headquarters of a media organization, the higher the level of consonance. Accuracy of information has also suffered as a result of cost-cutting. Reduced resources to research and confirm facts often lead to the release of not completely accurate news and content. Because of the concentration of media organizations, the effects of these errors are sometimes multiplied across several types of media.

The internet has helped to inject a level of participation in news commentary that did not exist in the past. This has taken the form of on-line polls of audiences and readership using customized software which operate at media Web sites. Although the samples reached in such polls are obviously not always representative, they are nevertheless a good beginning in getting the audience involved in developing opinions about issues. Current methods of polling offer audiences a limited number of choices, identified by the media, which may not always reflect the full spectrum of opinion. Perhaps more useful are facilities at certain Web sites for visitors to post their comments.

The Internet version of a phone-in comment is tremendously popular with interactive radio stations. A few international radio and television broadcasters have also started to use audience postings of comments at Web sites and e-mail, as a channel for the audience to participate in live panel discussions. The low cost of using the Internet by the audience permits this form of live participation at the global level on a sustained basis and, if facilitated effectively, will contribute towards enriching the diversity of perspectives in all types of media. In participation of a different sort, newsmakers now use the Internet to reach out directly to the audience, bypassing the media. Court judgements have been posted directly on to the Internet, as have copious copies of original reports of powerful government-appointed investigating authorities. Such events are being multiplied in a myriad of other events, ranging from the birth of a child to an expedition on Mount Everest.

Quick-thinking editors and their lawyers have found an interesting innovative use of the new technologies in the defence of the freedom of the media. United States media organizations subpoenaed for information in their possession, and faced with prospects of losing the legal challenge when no important information is involved, have been known to publish photographs or broadcast footages so that they can honestly claim that they have not surrendered any unpublished material to the prosecutors. The new technologies allow news stories and pictures to be rushed out into the public domain over the Internet. Television companies, faced with the need to place uninteresting and insignificant footage in the public domain, have been known to broadcast this material in the middle of the night using an idle satellite.

3

Universal Information Infrastructure

Universal access to the new information services and media is in many minds the most important of these principles, and is implicitly embodied in the Universal Declaration of Human Rights, particularly Article 19 bearing on freedom of expression and Article 27 relating to freedom of access to information and protection of users' security and privacy.

Governments, industry and the civil society are seeking to apply these long accepted principles to the electronic information environment, but these efforts are hampered by major difficulties and challenges, including the critical issue of how to ensure fair conditions for the developing countries which are entering the digital age at a major disadvantage.

At the same time, however, most of the national and international debates seem to be concentrating on the technological and economic aspects of information and communication technologies (ICTs), because of their more immediate perceived impact, perhaps to the detriment of the others which will ultimately have a deeper, more fundamental significance in achieving an Information Society for All. We therefore feel that this panel is a particularly timely forum to explore the "right of access to information" and national and international strategies by which information and knowledge resources can be developed as a global public good, stressing important "infoethical" issues.

At the most basic level, universal access means ensuring all citizens access to telecommunication services and other ICT facilities. Disparities and inequalities in Internet access - now commonly referred to as the "digital divide" - are considerable, particularly in developing countries where the Internet is most often far too expensive to be accessible to ordinary citizens and most public service institutions and is often available only in major population centres.

The case of Internet service connections, for which there is no regulation at the international level, and that of access to the underlying telecommunication channels which falls within the regulatory framework developed by the International Telecommunication Union (ITU).

In the telecom area, with the mounting pressure to abolish bilaterally negotiated cost sharing arrangements (the so-called "accounting rate" system of the ITU), developing countries will face an unprecedented burden to maintain their telecommunication systems.

The net result of this "rate re-balancing" is that the telecommunication operators in developing countries will be forced to offset the costs by increasing their national call charges which are often already very high relative to local means, particularly in rural areas, thus placing further constraints on access to knowledge resources for disadvantaged populations.

Solutions require balanced consideration by national and international regulators since the telecom privatisation and deregulation movement which is at the root of the these tendencies is also enabling many consumers in developing countries to access the Internet by leased line and dial-up access at reasonable prices, especially where monopoly public telecommunication operators had been inefficient or did not reinvest their high profits in infrastructure to improve access.

In another, but related, development, advanced technology, high speed Internet backbones and powerful network nodes, built up over a period of time, have led to an overwhelming concentration of Internet backbone business in one country, the USA.

Currently, even for intra-European networks, local Internet service providers (ISPs) often use Virginia as their international Internet hub, and the majority of ISPs in developing countries are linked to the US-based operators for intra-regional and sometimes even national, traffic. ISPs outside the USA must in most cases pay the entire costs of these two-way links, and ironically, under these circumstances, even the poorest countries are obliged to subsidize the Internet providers and users in the United States.

The issue of strengthening intra-regional networks, combining commercial and public service traffic, has to be brought forward high on the agendas of regional forums. Serious thought should be given to the possibility of establishing high capacity regional backbones to connect each country within a multi-hub global network in which nobody dominates connectivity - as is already under consideration, for example, within the Asia Pacific Economic Cooperation (APEC) forum.

Public service institutions in many developing countries - universities, research centres, libraries, museums, NGOs and government agencies - are facing special difficulties in participating in the information revolution because of economic and associated obstacles to access, particularly where the Internet has been developed mainly on a commercial basis as opposed to the situation in the industrialized countries where its origin was as a service to the academic and research communities.

The general idea of a "public service sector ICT consortium" can be useful in ensuring the access of public service institutions to networks and services. Such a consortium relies on the principle of self-help, drawing on the strengths of the different institutions to consolidate demand for services, to promote appropriate public policies, and to provide cost-effective support for training, infrastructure and content development. This approach is not about duplicating facilities of the private sector, but rather about complementarity and co-operation between the public and private sectors to ensure improvements in public services through ICTs.

Public service sector consortia can take many forms. One model which has been promoted by UNESCO and other UN agencies is the multipurpose community telecentre (MCT) - a shared, sustainable facility empowering local communities to service their information and ICT requirements to improve literacy campaigns, basic and non-formal education, government programmes and participatory development action, all within the framework of a viable business plan. The basic justification and strategies for public service sector consortia were developed some years ago in a joint study of the ITU and UNESCO1, but need to be reviewed and updated in view of new developments in technologies and networks.

National authorities, telecommunication operators and ISPs could promote development and future markets by establishing concessionary rates for Internet access in public service institutions such as schools, academic organizations and public libraries. Such schemes, sometimes known as "e-rates" have been successfully promoted by governments and regulatory agencies in several countries, most notably the USA. The idea of an "Internet tax" has been proposed in various forms and forums to the cross-subsidization necessary to ensure universal access to the Internet.

Perhaps even more important than physical access to telematics facilities is universal access to knowledge content, which is at the root of building a "Knowledge Society" based upon lifelong learning and basic human values and rights. Education and knowledge must be considered in this context as not simply advantages for personal and professional fulfilment, but also as social capital - "global public goods" which are the natural concern of public authorities as developed in a very interesting recent publication of UNDP.

The knowledge base for the future knowledge economy is being developed largely through publicly funded instruments such as universities and research grants, while the exploitation of knowledge to produce products has become mainly a concern of private industry. While it is true that industries increasingly do their own product research, it is also true that the publicly funded institutions produce the researchers, and publicly funded academic institutes continue to be the fountain of knowledge.

The challenge is to define new concepts and frameworks to promote the common public welfare while encouraging private initiative and protecting rightful economic interests. A key concept in this strategy is that of the electronic public domain - information free of copyright including classical literature, fundamental and indigenous knowledge, and the information and data of governments or produced with public funds at the national and international levels - which represents a vast world documentary heritage accessible to all, a window on national cultures and an invaluable support for education and cultural industries in developing countries.

Paradoxically, public domain information, which is free of copyright and belongs to everybody, is often not well enough known to potential contributors and users because of lack of interest in promoting it, no direct profit being expected due its very "public" nature. In order to ensure effective management of and access to this knowledge, the principles of free access to information in the public domain will have to be defined and promoted through appropriate public policies and international agreements, and the necessary public service infrastructures such as virtual libraries and archives appropriately developed.

Another important consideration is that of "fair use" of protected information and knowledge.Current law and practice generally allow free use of published information for research, study, reviewing and reporting, and fair access to electronic knowledge resources can be seen as a corollary to this fair use principle. The most forceful counter-arguments to extending the concept of fair use to the electronic domain come from publishers who note that electronic texts available on the Internet are not only storable but also can be duplicated and re-distributed at will, while the analogous printed materials are browsed either in a library or a bookshop and hence are less vulnerable to copyright infringements.

Therefore, pressure is mounting from publishers to tighten copyright laws and to make browsing protected works on screen, and sharing them through networks without permission, illegal. An example is the "sui generis" right which can accorded under European law to databases irrespective of their original content or literary value, but which has not been questioned by many developing countries and not generally extended into international practice.

Policing of such tightened laws will be problematic with the difficulties of proving how and where the material is obtained and with ample opportunities to make changes to electronic text. In extreme cases some preventive technological solutions such as disabling of printing can be applied. However, it would seem more fruitful to expand the definitions of "fair use" and to work to inculcate in the world's citizens "infoethics" principles of respect for intellectual property.

Protecting human dignity in the digital age

The Internet is indeed a new mass medium, but also differs qualitatively from the "traditional" media in the degree to which it permits individual as well as mass interaction, providing new possibilities for creativity, expression and provision of personal services while raising new dangers of exploitation of citizens.

The creation of an international rating and filtering system for Internet content has been proposed as an alternative to national legislation regulating online speech. But contrary to their original intent, such systems may actually facilitate governmental restrictions on Internet expression.

Additionally, rating and filtering schemes may prevent individuals from discussing controversial or unpopular topics, impose burdensome compliance costs on speakers, distort the fundamental cultural diversity of the Internet, enable invisible "upstream" filtering which can infringe on the rights to information of citizens worldwide, and eventually create a homogenized Internet dominated by large commercial interests. In order to avoid the undesirable effects of legal and technical solutions that seek to block the free flow of information, alternative educational approaches could be emphasized as less restrictive means of ensuring beneficial uses of the Internet.

National education systems and publicly funded projects will have major responsibilities in producing skilled and knowledgeable people who will become both producers and users of ICT based content. The increase in the use of technologies in business, government organizations, and communities of all kinds are also posing serious threats to our fundamental right privacy.

In addition to the risks associated with new economic activities (e.g. on-line banking or data mining for the personal information market), the anonymous nature of the Internet may facilitate personnel harassment or "cyberstalking" which is becoming an increasing concern in some countries, as well as impersonation by unauthorized use of someone else's email address.

The focus of the global information society, with its intelligent networks, micro processors and ability to access massive reservoirs of knowledge has for the most part been on commerce and trade related issues. It is essential to consider the significance of information technology for human development and the "social capital" of knowledge.

Although the social, educational, ethical and cultural needs of our communities are intimately linked with economic welfare, it is essential to see the digital technology and the advent of global networks as offering much more than the means of doing e-business. This same technology can address many other vital human needs and support initiatives to improve education, research and knowledge levels and to deliver community services and an enormous range of public benefits.

A practical measure to achieve these goals is to expand the amount of, and improve access to, what is known as "public domain" information or "public content". Another way of thinking about public domain is to think in terms of rights to access information. Funding is a separate matter.

The link between access to information and economic welfare will in the near future become so significant that if the gap between the information rich and the information poor widens too far (whether as between communities or countries), there could be increased risk of global instability and negative impacts which reach well beyond local or national boundaries.

All countries have a vital interest in the development of a global information society and in the benefits that flow from a better informed and more knowledgeable population.

A government which promotes public content is an open government and therefore more likely to encourage greater participation by its citizens and to believe in greater transparency and accountability for decision-making. This is one way of encouraging citizens to participate in an information society. An informed population can contribute to debate, make their views known on issues and influence outcomes. These forces are a very powerful incentive for citizens; the various FOI (freedom of information) models can both encourage and empower citizens to participate in accessing and generating information.

The people's welfare will be better served through access to or disclosure of information, rather than a paternalistic approach where decisions are made on behalf of the people without informing or consulting them. One of the critical challenges is the tension between social objectives and the other economic interests in controlling or restricting the availability of certain types of information. This economic interest manifests as the intellectual property ("IP") rights of the content provider, author, inventor or other "owner" of the information.

However, the expansion of IP rights needs to be kept in check while the economics and impacts of other stakeholder interests are considered. There are specific ways to improve the balance of interests; for example, ensuring a limited duration of IP monopoly rights. In some jurisdictions, it is not possible to have copyright in a fact, only in an expression of an idea or in the particular compilation of the facts or a format.

There have always been a number of categories of exemptions from IP protections. For example: for human rights (eg freedom of the press); for public interest reasons; for library or archive deposits; for education and under special rules for non-profit institutions; under competition law; to adapt the law to new circumstances, as technology develops; and, for perceived market failure.

Many legal systems then apply various tests or factors as a guide to whether or not a proposed use will fall within these statutory categories of fair use. The scope of the fair use exception is unclear and so it has been left to the courts in many jurisdictions to define the boundaries of what amounts to fair use and is therefore non-infringing.

The origin of the fair use exception is directly relevant to the concepts underlying the public domain. Copyright is intended to advance learning and knowledge by creating an incentive system to induce authors to create and disseminate their works. However, the fair use exception is a more direct intervention or redistribution of rights to ensure access and equity for some socially beneficial purposes.

One of the most significant IP developments in the digital era is the automated rights management technology (ARM) or digital copyright management systems (CMS). These include technologies to monitor and track the exchange of digital information, such as payment per use for encrypted documents and software applications embedded in the information being accessed over the Net to ensure that the user pays for accessing protected information.

ARM technology will have a radical impact on the enforcement of IP rights in digital media and on the scope of fair use doctrine. Instead of seeking protection through very cumbersome and expensive copyright actions, the author (or content provider) can resort to the technology to ensure protection and rely on standardised one-to-one or bilateral licence contracts to ensure payment for use. This enables the content provider to by-pass the public law of copyright and to impose restrictions on the re-use of the information, irrespective of the application of the fair use doctrine.

The use of ARM technology could reduce transaction costs for copyrighted material. The result may be net economic benefits in the efficiencies of ARM because of the long term effect of pushing access prices down. It can be argued that the effects of ARM increase the value of copyrighted works and encourages greater production and improved distribution.

While this trend may benefit consumers by improving both the quality of and access to this information, there is still an issue for those that are concerned with the need for direct and immediate access to certain categories of information through the public domain; it is unknown how much of this licensed information will fall into the public domain. It is therefore very important to resist any further erosion of the fair use exception.

The new IP rights management technology is making it relatively inexpensive to control the boundaries of digital IP rights. Current policing methods, through registration and court action, are so costly and cumbersome that asserting private ownership (through the use of licensing contracts) may become a more efficient method of managing our society's creative and cultural resources.

The economic effects of these efficiencies need to be analysed in terms of their social and long term impacts on the availability of information in the public domain. There is also a trend by the courts to narrow the fair use doctrine as it applies to online information where it can be argued that a new ARM licensing regime establishes a market for that information. This judicial trend undermines the original social benefit bargain implicit in the fair use exception and in the other constraints on copyright protection.

There are numerous instances where information rights are not exclusive; for example, where personal information is held about an individual. This may give rise to a privacy right to access that information or constrain its subsequent re-use, even though another may regard that same information as intellectual property. There are many precedents where the law recognises shared interests and allows modified or limited entitlements. It is essential to retain the mechanisms of fair use and to address the public benefit of having relatively unrestrained access to certain categories of information.

The widespread use of digital ARM technology, will pre-empt fair use and abrogate the balance which most copyright laws seek to achieve. This is why the fair use doctrine needs to be developed in a way that could equally be applied to private contract or licensing regimes.

The fair use doctrine, adapted, clarified and modified from public copyright law, could be another such example of public good or benefit or welfare, requiring articulation in our IP treaties and laws at both international and national level. By commodifying information and promoting a private law (contract) regime for digital content, we narrow our vision to assessing value purely in individual preference and neo-classical market terms.

This fails to appreciate the impact of knowledge development and progress, and ignores other means of valuation, such as whether overall value can be realised for society. There is much work being done on developing other economic models for valuing information, which challenge current presumptions, and are worthy of exploration.

The protection and enforcement of intellectual property rights should contribute to the promotion of technological innovation and to the transfer and dissemination of technology, to the mutual advantage of producers and users of technological knowledge and in a manner conducive to social and economic welfare, and to the balance of rights and obligations. This means that the recognition and enforcement of intellectual property rights can be subject to higher social values and, in particular, that a balance needs to be found with other users of technological knowledge.

New technologies developed by the defence industry are spreading into law enforcement, civilian agencies, and private companies. At the same time, outdated laws and regulations are failing to check an expanding pattern of abuses. It is now common wisdom that the power, capacity and speed of information technology are accelerating rapidly. The extent of privacy invasion - or certainly the potential to invade privacy increases correspondingly. .But it is not merely the increased capacity and decreasing cost of information technology that creates threats to privacy.

Globalisation of systems such as the internet removes geographical limitations to the flow of data. Convergence is leading to the elimination of technological barriers between systems. Modern information systems are increasingly interoperable with other systems, and can mutually exchange and process different forms of data. Meanwhile, the phenomenon of multi-media, which fuses many forms of transmission and expression of data and images, creates vast difficulties for legislators wishing to protect personal privacy.

Governments and private sector organisations have moved in recent years to incorporate surveillance into almost every aspect of our finances, communication and lifestyle. While paying lip service to privacy, they argue that surveillance is necessary to maintain law and order and to create economic efficiency. The rationale is often self serving, and somewhat bogus, but a substantial number of people have nevertheless been persuaded that the surrender of privacy is the price we must pay for a better and safer society.

Throughout the past quarter century, no other fundamental right in the arena of public policy has generated such turbulence and controversy. And yet, as one writer has observed "privacy is the right from which all other rights derive". It is central to the freedom and autonomy of people, and it is perhaps the key factor that limits the power of the State. Torture, discrimination, racial hatred: these issues have achieved baseline consensus within the international community. Privacy, however, is viewed by many governments and corporations as the bogeyman of human rights. It is conventional wisdom amongst many organisations that privacy of the individual and the protection of personal information impedes economic performance and law enforcement.

Access to Networks and Services

Access to information is a critical input for rural areas, in addition to its long-term implications in human development. This is not just a problem for rural inhabitants, but rather a public concern of the whole society. In any service, Universal Access roots on three multi-layered regulatory principia:

1) Geographical coverage, to bring it to every community.
2) Affordability -reasonable prices respect to the income of the users.
3) Equitability -same opportunities to all regions and social groups.

The objective of Integrated Development implies maximum values for all such dimensions, and the regulatory framework acts as an intermediate layer between commercial and group interests, and the moral obligation to promote it.

The coverage depends on the size and the capillarity of the network, but experience in developing countries has shown that even a huge investment effort to expand the system is not enough per se: moreover, a strong growth in the overall teledensity may mask increasing regional inequalities and rural-urban teledensity gaps.

Therefore, equitability is also a goal for Universal Access, since public telecommunications systems are supposed to perform balancing roles in the development of the economy. A particular access policy can drive rural-urban gaps either to exacerbation, to statu-quo or to regression phases. The effectiveness of Universal Access regulation depends on how close to the needs put by the Integrated Development layer can it drive the natural action of market forces and interest groups.

Typical complaints from Internet users in South America are low speed, scarcity of local content, low security and high prices. It is important to keep track of income disparities among regions and social groups, even in the same country.

Usually, expenditures in telecommunications services should be limited to about 1 to 3% of the total income, in order to yield a net increment in the social welfare of individuals, so a typical household in Santiago will find difficult to afford even a PSTN lifeline subscription. In communities without local ISPs, dial-up sessions require expensive long distance calls, almost impossible to afford. Others with just a small provider often do not benefit from discounts or special rates. Conversely, Internet users in large cities obtain better prices and higher quality of service, due to strong competition and more connectivity options.

In 1994, during the First World Telecommunications Development Conference in Argentina, UNESCO and the ITU submitted the joint document: "The right to communicate: at what price?" It´s worth reading it again, as a start point in successive policy proposals submitted by international organizations to foster Universal Access. The 1999 Report on the Internet from the ITU has specific recommendations to promote the industry, to build infrastructure, to expand access, to stimulate usage and creation of local content, and to promote competition in the access market.

Many countries are actively working in these issues. For example, there are several programs to facilitate public access to information through public libraries, schools and community telecenters.

In another policy toolkit, drawn from the Informatics Initiative 2000 Conference for the Americas -promoted two years ago by the Inter-American Development Bank- again there are recommendations to extend access via community telecenters, as well as special e-rates for schools, libraries and healthcare.

Universal Access to Information is largely more than a matter of regulation. It requires a strong involvement of the private sector and local institutions of the communities. There are a number of large projects with government funding, like in Canada, Australia and the USA, but also good experiences born in communities, like in Hungary, Estonia, Western Australia and the United Kingdom, while Internet access projects in Ghana and Peru are rather based on entrepreneurship and franchising.

The largest potentially suitable access networks in every country include the schools, the post offices, the public libraries, the FM radios, the cable TV providers and lately, the community telecenters. Government support is often necessary, but is not a guarantee for a smart allocation of resources.

The marginal impact of public access to information is inversely depending on the size and the resources already available in the community. Provided that every facility will require a minimum number of users and a sort of balance between affordability and sustainability, the usefulness of public access points tends to increase for small, distant and low-income communities, with little exposure to technology and to alternative information sources.

Encryption and information infrastructure

A variety of "key recovery," "key escrow," and "trusted third-party" encryption requirements have been suggested in recent years by government agencies seeking to conduct covert surveillance within the changing environments brought about by new technologies. This report examines the fundamental properties of these requirements and attempts to outline the technical risks, costs, and implications of deploying systems that provide government access to encryption keys.

The deployment of key-recovery-based encryption infrastructures to meet law enforcement's stated specifications will result in substantial sacrifices in security and greatly increased costs to the end-user. Building the secure computer-communication infrastructures necessary to provide adequate technological underpinnings demanded by these requirements would be enormously complex and is far beyond the experience and current competency of the field. Even if such infrastructures could be built, the risks and costs of such an operating environment may ultimately prove unacceptable. In addition, these infrastructures would generally require extraordinary levels of human trustworthiness.

These difficulties are a function of the basic government access requirements proposed for key-recovery encryption systems. They exist regardless of the design of the recovery systems -whether the systems use private-key cryptography or public-key cryptography; whether the databases are split with secret-sharing techniques or maintained in a single hardened secure facility; whether the recovery services provide private keys, session keys, or merely decrypt specific data as needed; and whether there is a single centralized infrastructure, many decentralized infrastructures, or a collection of different approaches.

All key-recovery systems require the existence of a highly sensitive and highly-available secret key or collection of keys that must be maintained in a secure manner over an extended time period. These systems must make decryption information quickly accessible to law enforcement agencies without notice to the key owners. These basic requirements make the problem of general key recovery difficult and expensive - and potentially too insecure and too costly for many applications and many users.

Attempts to force the widespread adoption of key-recovery encryption through export controls, import or domestic use regulations, or international standards should be considered in light of these factors. The public must carefully consider the costs and benefits of embracing government-access key recovery before imposing the new security risks and spending the huge investment required (potentially many billions of dollars, in direct and indirect costs) to deploy a global key recovery infrastructure.

A collaborative effort to study the technical implications of controversial proposals by the United States and other national governments to deploy large-scale "key recovery" systems that provide third-party access to decryption keys. Insofar as is possible, we have considered the impact of these policies without regard to individual encryption schemes or particular government proposals. Rather, we have attempted to look broadly at the essential elements of key recovery needed to fulfill the expressed requirements of governments (as distinct from the features that encryption users might desire). This report considers the general impact of meeting the government's requirements rather than the merits of any particular key recovery system or proposal that meets them. Our analysis is independent of whether the key-recovery infrastructure is centralized or widely distributed.

We have specifically chosen not to endorse, condemn, or draw conclusions about any particular regulatory or legislative proposal or commercial product. Rather, it is our hope that our findings will shed further light on the debate over key recovery and provide a long-needed baseline analysis of the costs of key recovery as policymakers consider embracing one of the most ambitious and far-reaching technical deployments of the information age.

Although there are many aspects to the debate on the proper role of encryption and key recovery in a free society, we have chosen to focus entirely on the technical issues associated with this problem rather than on more general political or social questions. Indeed, many have suggested that the very notion of a pervasive government key recovery infrastructure runs counter to the basic principles of freedom and privacy in a democracy and that alone is reason enough to avoid deploying such systems. This reasoning is independent of whether the key-recovery infrastructure is centralized or widely distributed. The technical nature of our analysis should not be interpreted as an endorsement of the social merits of government key recovery; in fact, we encourage vigorous public debate on this question.

Encryption and the Global Information Infrastructure

The Global Information Infrastructure promises to revolutionize electronic commerce, reinvigorate government, and provide new and open access to the information society. Yet this promise cannot be achieved without information security and privacy. Without a secure and trusted infrastructure, companies and individuals will become increasingly reluctant to move their private business or personal information online.

The need for information security is widespread and touches all of us, whether users of information technology or not. Sensitive information of all kinds is increasingly finding its way into electronic form. Examples include:

— Private personal and business communications, including telephone conversations, FAX messages, and electronic mail;

— Electronic funds transfers and other financial transactions;

— Sensitive business information and trade secrets;

Data used in the operation of critical infrastructure systems such as air traffic control, the telephone network, or the power grid; and Health records, personnel files, and other personal information.

Electronically managed information touches almost every aspect of daily life in modern society. This rising tide of important yet unsecured electronic data leaves our society increasingly vulnerable to curious neighbours, industrial spies, rogue nations, organized crime, and terrorist organizations.

Paradoxically, although the technology for managing and communicating electronic information is improving at a remarkable rate, this progress generally comes at the expense of intrinsic security. In general, as information technology improves and becomes faster, cheaper, and easier to use, it becomes less possible to control (or even identify) where sensitive data flows, where documents originated, or who is at the other end of the telephone. The basic communication infrastructure of our society is becoming less secure, even as we use it for increasingly vital purposes. Cryptographic techniques more and more frequently will become the only viable approach to assuring the privacy and safety of sensitive information as these trends continue.

Encryption is an essential tool in providing security in the information age. Encryption is based on the use of mathematical procedures to scramble data so that it is extremely difficult -if not virtually impossible -for anyone other than authorized recipients to recover the original "plaintext." Properly implemented encryption allows sensitive information to be stored on insecure computers or transmitted across insecure networks. Only parties with the correct decryption "key" (or keys) are able to recover the plaintext information.

Highly secure encryption can be deployed relatively cheaply, and it is widely believed that encryption will be broadly adopted and embedded in most electronic communications products and applications for handling potentially valuable data. Applications of cryptography include protecting files from theft or unauthorized access, securing communications from interception, and enabling secure business transactions. Other cryptographic techniques can be used to guarantee that the contents of a file or message have not been altered (integrity), to establish the identity of a party (authentication), or to make legal commitments (non-repudiation).

In making information secure from unwanted eavesdropping, interception, and theft, strong encryption has an ancillary effect: it becomes more difficult for law enforcement to conduct certain kinds of surreptitious electronic surveillance (particularly wiretapping) against suspected criminals without the knowledge and assistance of the target. This difficulty is at the core of the debate over key recovery.

Key Recovery

Requirements and proposals

The United States and other national governments have sought to prevent widespread use of cryptography unless "key recovery" mechanisms guaranteeing law enforcement access to plaintext are built into these systems. The requirements imposed by such government-driven key recovery systems are different from the features sought by encryption users, and ultimately impose substantial new risks and costs. Key recovery encryption systems provide some form of access to plaintext outside of the normal channel of encryption and decryption. Key recovery is sometimes also called "key escrow."

The term "escrow" became popular in connection with the U.S. government's Clipper Chip initiative, in which a master key to each encryption device was held "in escrow" for release to law enforcement. Today the term "key recovery" is used as generic term for these systems, encompassing the various "key escrow," "trusted third-party," "exceptional access," "data recovery," and "key recovery" encryption systems introduced in recent years. Although there are differences between these systems, the distinctions are not critical for our purposes. In this report, the general term "key recovery" is used in a broad sense, to refer to any system for assuring third-party (government) access to encrypted data. Key recovery encryption systems work in a variety of ways.

Early "key escrow" proposals relied on the storage of private keys by the U.S. government, and more recently by designated private entities. Other systems have "escrow agents" or "key recovery agents" that maintain the ability to recover the keys for a particular encrypted communication session or stored file; these systems require that such "session keys" be encrypted with a key known by a recovery agent and included with the data. Some systems split the ability to recover keys among several agents. Many interested parties have sought to draw sharp distinctions among the various key recovery proposals. It is certainly true that several new key recovery systems have emerged that can be distinguished from the original "Clipper" proposal by their methods of storing and recovering keys. However, our discussion takes a higher-level view of the basic requirements of the problem rather than the details of any particular scheme; it does not require a distinction between "key escrow," "trusted third-party," and "key recovery." All these systems share the essential elements that concern us for the purposes of this study:

— A mechanism, external to the primary means of encryption and decryption, by which a third party can obtain covert access to the plaintext of encrypted data.

— The existence of a highly sensitive secret key (or collection of keys) that must be secured for an extended period of time.

Taken together, these elements encompass a system of "ubiquitous key recovery" designed to meet law enforcement specifications. While some specific details may change, the basic requirements most likely will not: they are the essential requirements for any system that meets the stated objective of guaranteeing law enforcement agencies timely access, without user notice, to the plaintext of encrypted communications traffic.

Key recoverability

Key recovery systems have gained currency due to the desire of government intelligence and law enforcement agencies to guarantee that they have access to encrypted information without the knowledge or consent of encryption users. A properly designed cryptosystem makes it essentially impossible to recover encrypted data without knowledge of the correct key. In some cases this creates a potential problem for the users of encryption themselves; the cost of keeping unauthorized parties out is that if keys are lost or unavailable at the time they are needed, the owners of the encrypted data will be unable to make use of their own information. It has been suggested, therefore, that industry needs and wants key recovery, and that the kind of key recovery infrastructure promoted by the government would serve the commercial world's needs for assuring availability of its own encrypted data.

Several recent government proposals (along with commercial products and services designed to meet the government's requirements) have been promoted as serving the dual role of assuring government access as well as "owner" access to encrypted data. However, the requirements of a government and the requirements of the commercial world and individual users are very different in this regard, so different that, in fact, there is little overlap between systems that address these two problems.

The ultimate goal of government-driven key recovery encryption, as stated in the U.S. Department of Commerce's recent encryption regulations, "envisions a worldwide key management infrastructure with the use of key escrow and key recovery encryption items." The requirements put forward to meet law enforcement demands for such global key recovery systems include:

Third-party/government access without notice to or consent of the user. Even so-called "self-escrow" systems, where companies might hold their own keys, are required to provide sufficient insulation between the recovery agents and the key owners to avoid revealing when decryption information has been released.

Key recovery helps law enforcement only if it is so widespread that it is used for the bulk of encrypted stored information and communications, whether or not there is end-user demand for a recovery feature. High-availability, around-the-clock access to plain-text under a variety of operational conditions. Law enforcement seeks the ability to obtain decryption keys quickly - within two hours under current U.S. and other proposed regulations. Few commercial encryption users need the ability to recover lost keys around the clock, or on such short notice.

Access to encrypted communications traffic as well as to encrypted stored data. To the extent that there is commercial demand for key recovery, it is limited to stored data rather than communications traffic.

In fact, the requirements of government key recovery are almost completely incompatible with those of commercial encryption users. The differences are especially acute in four areas: the kinds of data for which recovery is required, the kinds of keys for which recovery is required, the manner in which recoverable keys are managed, and the relationship between key certification and key recovery. Government key recovery does not serve private and business users especially well; similarly, the key management and key recoverability systems naturally arising in the commercial world do not adapt well to serve a government.

Communication Traffic vs. Stored Data

While key "recoverability" is a potentially important added-value feature in certain stored data systems, in other applications of cryptography there is little or no user demand for this feature. In particular, there is hardly ever a reason for an encryption user to want to recover the key used to protect a communication.

4

Educational Approach in ICTs

Information and communications technologies (ICT) are a diverse set of technological tools and resources used to communicate, and to create, disseminate, store, and manage information. Communication and information are at the very heart of the educational process, consequently ICT-use in education has a long history. ICT has played an educational role in formal and non-formal settings, in programs provided by governmental agencies, public and private educational institutions, for-profit corporations and non-profit groups, and secular and religious communities. Much has been written about the use of film, radio, telephones, and television in education. Because access to digital tools, applications, and networks continues to grow worldwide and media are increasingly available in digital form, ICT-use in education can be expected to increase dramatically.

Education worldwide is facing a significant challenge in preparing students and teachers for "our future 'knowledge-based' society" during a time when most teachers are not prepared to use ICT and "the majority of existing school buildings, even in the most developed countries, are not equipped to integrate the new information and communication technologies." In this chapter, we focus on "new" digital ICTs with special emphasis on educational uses of the Internet and the World Wide Web. Several important issues in respect to the use of ICTs in educational settings including how newer ICTs differ from older technologies, why these differences are thought to be educationally important, what research shows about the effectiveness of ICTs in education, what measures are being taken to create ICT-enabled learning environments, and some of the significant issues facing educators and policy-makers when considering implementing ICT.

Although our focus will be on formal education, we will also refer to the use of ICT in non-formal and informal education. Along the way, we will provide a few of the innumerable possible examples of current educational ICT applications. To illuminate trends that will help readers to understand current directions and promising practices in the application of these systems in educational settings. However, although digital ICTs are quickly becoming more accessible, it is important to note that earlier ICTs continue to play a critical role in education worldwide. Access to films, videotapes, telephones, television or radio is still far more commonplace than access to a computer or the Internet and World Wide Web. For example, the Telesecundaria in Mexico, which began in 1965 as a closed-circuit pilot, today delivers classes designed for lower secondary school level to over 12,000 rural communities enrolling more than 800,000 students. The Mexican government plans to open an additional 4,500 Telesecundaria schools enrolling

250,000 more students between 1998 and 2002. The China TV University system enrolls over half a million students in degree programs and graduates over 100,000 per year.

The new digital ICTs are not single technologies but combinations of hardware, software, media, and delivery systems. Today, ICT in education encompasses a great range of rapidly evolving technologies such as desktop, notebook, and handheld computers; digital cameras; local area networking; the Internet and the World Wide Web; CD-ROMs and DVDs; and applications such as word processors, spreadsheets, tutorials, simulations, electronic mail (email), digital libraries, computer-mediated conferencing, videoconferencing, and virtual reality. It should also be noted that use of newer ICTs is being integrated with use of older technologies. For example, it is not uncommon to find textbooks sold with CD-ROMs containing multimedia materials or links to related websites. An exhaustive review of all of these technologies, combinations of technologies, and applications is not possible here. We also acknowledge the difficulties in implementing such innovations, and we are sensitive to the fact that whatever is said now about ICTs in education will quickly become outdated as the technologies and educational applications continue to rapidly evolve.

Changes in Communications and Information Industries

Our emphasis on digital ICT tools and applications in education mirrors profound structural changes occurring worldwide in communications and information industries. The ability to digitize analog signals and transmit them over telecommunications networks is resulting in the restructuring of the radio, telephone, television, publishing, entertainment, and computer industries into new multimedia industries that create digital products combining voice, video, text, graphics, images, and animations, and deliver these signals electronically. An example of this trend can be found in Hong Kong where New World Telephone is installing "PowerPhones" from which users may read or send electronic mail, send a fax, search online multimedia directories about hotels and tourist spots, and make a telephone call. Another example is Internet 'telephony' software that now makes it possible to place domestic and international calls from a computer to any telephone anywhere in the world.

ICT Access Worldwide

Our emphasis also mirrors the increasing access to digital tools and resources worldwide. Although estimating the number of people with Internet access is difficult at best, one current estimate places the total number at around 150 million in late 1998, an increase of over 60% since early 1997. Internet access is at present strongly concentrated in a small number of countries, providing services to a fraction of the world's population: over 90% of Internet hosts are located in the world's richest 29 counties.

However, this may be expected to change over time as telecommunications costs continue to drop precipitously and governments deregulate access. For example, the number of Internet users in India is expected to climb from half a million in 1998 to 1.5 million by the year 2000. In Africa, it is estimated that there currently are between 800,000 and 1 million Internet users. The current ratio of Internet users to people in Africa is estimated to be one for every 5,000 compared to a world average of about one Internet user to every 40 people. But here, too, the situation is rapidly changing. In 1996, only 16 countries in Africa had Internet access. Now, 53 (three-fourths) of the capital cities are online and the rest will soon follow.

A number of international infrastructure building initiatives are underway on the continent including the United Nations Secretary General's programme Harnessing Information Technology for Development that will substantially improve the Internet infrastructure by the year 2000. The Russian Non-Profit Center for Internet Technologies estimates that there are now about one million Russians online and that this number is doubling every year. And, in the next two years, the number of Internet users in Latin America is expected to grow from 8.5 million to about 34 million. The number of Latin American websites, most of which are operated by businesses, could triple in the next year to over 500,000. In Asia, estimates place the total number of Chinese online in Hong Kong, Taiwan, and Singapore at 2.6 million. The number of users in China almost doubled (620,000 - 1.175 million) from late 1997 to mid-June, 1998. Some estimates predict there will be 20 million Internet users in China by the year 2000. As these few examples help illustrate, although ICT access is still chiefly available to citizens of developed countries; such access is fast becoming possible in developing countries worldwide.

Although no comprehensive data on ICT in schools worldwide apparently exists, it is clear from many national examples that schools are also increasingly being equipped with ICT. It is also apparent that ICT equipment and Internet connectivity is still much more abundant in North American schools than elsewhere. In the United States, the ratio of students per computer dropped from 63:1 to 6:1 from 1985 to 1997 while the number of schools with internet access has grown from 35% in 1994 to 72% in 1997. In Africa, the Creating Learning Networks for African Teachers, part of the UN's Harnessing Information Technology for Development initiative mentioned above, will equip a maximum of four teacher training colleges (TTCs) in each of 20 African countries with a computer and full access to the Internet. The teacher training curriculum development and the creation of 20 national educational WWW sites. In Europe, more than 80% of schools in Solvenia have access to the Internet - 93% of secondary schools and 80% of primary schools—which is similar to the percentages of developed countries. Nearly two-thirds of secondary schools have a website.

In the United Kingdom, the pupil to computer ratio is 16:1 in primary schools and 9:1 in secondary schools, while 43% of schools in the United Kingdom are connected to the Internet. The British Government plans to connect all schools, colleges, universities, libraries, and as many community centers as possible to the Internet by 2002. In Germany, the Schulen ans Netz initiative begun in 1996, will connect 10,000 schools to the Internet by mid-1999. As of late 1997, of approximately 6,500 were connected and 1,700 had their own website. And in Italy, a national program in 1995 resulted in 120 schools being supplied with multimedia equipment. Last year, plans were announced for the installation of computer and multimedia facilities in 15,000 Italian schools to be carried out by the year 2000. At the end of the programme, approximately 25% of all Italian state schools will have access to on-line facilities and the Internet and will be equipped with advanced hardware and multimedia educational software.

In Asia, similar developments are taking place. In Japan, as of 1997, over 94% of pubic schools were computer-equipped and 10% were connected to the Internet. The Government plans to provide a pupil to computer ratio of 2:1 in middle schools and 1:1 in high schools by 1999. All of the public schools in Japan will be connected to the Internet by 2003. In the People's Republic of China, the central government will increase funding for basic, vocational and higher education over the next two years. These plans include strategies to make increasing use of Internet-based educational programs. In South America, in 1993, the Chilean government established the Enlaces (Links) to connect schools and related institutions to Chile's national computer network. By 1996, over180 primary schools and 62 secondary schools had been connected and, by the year 2000, the Chilean government plans to have 50% of the 8,250 primary schools and 100% of the 1,700 secondary schools connected. The Enlaces initiative also includes equipping schools with computers and a combination of locally produced educational software and commercial products that are available in Spanish language versions.

These few examples serve to illustrate that efforts to provide ICT and Internet access to teachers and students in developed and developing countries around the world can be expected to continue and accelerate until most, if not all, schools are equipped and connected in the next century.

ICT access in informal and non-formal education

Informal and non-formal education refers to educational activities and programs that are offered outside of formal educational institutions, including those offered by libraries, museums, community schools and centers, zoos, planetariums, commercial companies, and many other organizations. Informal and non-formal education institutions, too, are increasingly being equipped with ICT and connected to the Internet. At present, about 20% of libraries in the United Kingdom are connected to the Internet. The British government's National Grid for Learning initiative will connect all British libraries and museums to the Internet. In the United States, a 1998 survey sponsored by the American Library Association found 73% of the nation's public libraries offered basic Internet access to the public.

Many public and privately funded museums are offering ICT-based learning opportunities. For example, the Computer Museum's website offers activities designed to help individuals learn about computers. The British Natural History Museum, as part of a European Union funded to enable multimedia applications such as virtual museums and galleries to be accessed from remote locations, has constructed a virtual model of the Endeavour, Captain Cook's (an English explorer) ship. The ship, as well as virtual reality objects of seabirds and other animals encountered by Cooke on his voyages, are available on the Web. And, in a joint with the Fraunhofer Institute for Software and Systems Engineering, the German Historical Museum in Berlin and the Haus der Geschichte of the Federal Republic of Germany in Bonn are developing a virtual exhibition of German history for the Internet. Community school efforts, too, are increasingly making use of ICTs. The Lighthouse in Thailand is offering non-formal educational programs at five locations in Thailand as well as an online 'community magazine'. The community school-based initiates a challenge against the existing educational system ... The new environments and new technologies will be the main mechanism to help learners generate their own ideas, expand them, and share them with others".

ICTs are rapidly becoming available for use in every setting. This trend is true for formal, informal, and non-formal teaching and learning programs. However, such access is much more common among the rich, and in the developed countries, than for the poor, or in developing countries.

In part, efforts to connect educational organizations to the Internet are being driven by societal pressure. But such efforts are also being driven from within education by powerful differences between older and new ICTs, differences that greatly enhance the usefulness of such technologies to teaching and learning. New ICTs differ in several important dimensions from older technologies, including the integration of multiple media, interactivity, flexibility of use, and connectivity. Understanding these differences will?6 provide a clearer picture of why the use of ICT in education can be expected to continue to grow.

Integration of multiple media

Because of advances in digital technologies, it is now possible to integrate multiple media into single educational applications. Multimedia applications on CD-ROMs and websites may incorporate text, pictures, audio, graphics, animations, simulations, full-motion video, and links to other software or websites greatly enriching the learning experience. For example, Astronomy Village: Investigating the Universe is a CDROM-based multimedia program developed at the NASA Classroom of the Future that contains ten complete four-week-long investigations for secondary students. Multimedia tools available on the CD-ROM include an image-processing program, an image browser, a telecommunications program for accessing the World Wide Web, a star life cycle simulator, an orbital simulator, and a 3-D star simulator. Multimedia resources include 85 minutes of digitized video clips; more than 300 images from the Hubble Space Telescope and other instruments; 12 illustrated audio lectures by astronomers discussing their work; over 100 computer animations and graphics; and 180 full text documents such as book chapters, NASA publications, and articles from astronomy journals and magazines.

Interactivity

Earlier technologies used for instruction were passive in nature. That is, the delivery of instruction required no action on the part of students beyond listening, watching, and perhaps taking notes. Such ICTs were one-way channels of instructional delivery. New ICTs give the student and teacher the ability to control, manipulation, and contribute to the information environment. On the lowest and least valuable level, this may simply mean the student controls the pace and order of a presentation. But much more is possible. Using ICT students may not only make choices about the pace and order of a presentation, but may choose topics; take notes; answer questions; explore virtual landscapes; enter, draw or chart data; run simulated experiments; create and manipulate images; make their own multimedia presentations, communicate with others, and more. Previously, ICT-use required students to be grouped together in a controlled environment at a specific time and location. With some technologies, for example radio and television, use was rigidly tied to schedules developed by people far removed from the day-to-day functioning of the classroom.

New ICT applications have given rise to the term 'anytime-anyplace,' a reflection of the flexibility possible in using ICT to support teaching and learning. The outgrowth of this flexibility has been the development of 'virtual' educational experiences. A virtual experience refers to educational situations in which distance and time separate the teacher and students, who use ICT to interactively to share resources, communicate, and learn. Virtual education allows students to study at their own time, place and pace. In essence, a virtual education means having educational transactions accessible?7 from the home, workplace, or anywhere that the student chooses to be. Virtual classrooms, schools, colleges, and universities offering classes by email, computer-mediated conferencing (CMC), videoconferencing, or websites, or combinations of these technologies, are proliferating.

Perhaps the most powerful feature of new ICTs is connectivity. Prior to the 1990s, computers in educational settings were seldom connected to local area networks (LANs) or the Internet. With the widespread adoption of LANs, decreasing telecommunications costs, increasing bandwidth, and the invention of the World Wide Web, educational access to the Internet is becoming commonplace. If equipped with a computer, appropriate software, and Internet access, students and teachers have access to every other person on the planet who has an Internet account, hundreds of thousands of information archives, and millions of webpages of educationally relevant content. These four dimensions - integration of multiple media, interactivity, flexibility of use, and connectivity - distinguish digital ICT from previous technologies. Because of these differences, educators are finding powerful new ways to integrate digital ICTs into the curricula.

Effectiveness

Perhaps the most important question about ICT is how effective is its use in education? To answer this question one must consider three aspects. How effective is ICT-mediated instruction when compared to traditional face-to-face instruction? What does ICT enable that would not otherwise be possible? And third, are ICT worth their costs?

ICT-mediated instruction

The effectiveness of ICT in education is what, if any, impact ICT-mediated instruction has on student performance. ICT-mediated instruction refers to instruction delivered via a technological channel such as television, radio, or a computer and network. ICT-mediated instruction can be synchronous, with both the instructor and the student participating simultaneously. For example, instruction may be delivered via desktop videoconferencing by a teacher located at a university to employees at widely separated companies. ICT-mediated instruction may also be delivered asynchronously, with the instructor and student participating at different times.

Instruction based on teaching materials placed on a website does not requiring simultaneous participation. Or synchronicity may not matter, as when self-contained instructional materials are packaged on a CD-ROM. In this case, the instructional designer may have developed the materials months or even years before the student uses them and communication between the two is impossible. Early studies of ICT-mediated instruction's effect on student learning have been characterized as the "no significant difference" phenomena. That is to say, whatever medium of instructional delivery - film, radio, television, telephone, or computer—was used, no significant difference on performance measures was found between students receiving ICT-mediated instruction and those receiving traditional face-to-face instruction in a classroom. Both groups perform equally well. Studies focusing on the use of computer-mediated instruction conducted in the 1980s found more positive results. In a meta-analysis of over 500 individual studies.

Sudies of computer use prior to the 1990s. Such use was often limited to drill and practice and tutorial software programs. In the 1990s, use of ICT in schools is moving toward engaging students in "authentic" learning tasks in which students use computers, software, and network access to simulate events, communicate, collaborate, analyze data and access information resources. For these applications of ICT in schools, the research data are less extensive. However, some individual studies have been conducted that demonstrate positive learning and affective outcomes. A recent study by ETS of student achievement in mathematics and the use of ICT -the first such study to document relationships between student use of technology across the United States and higher scores on a national standardized test - concluded that "technology does matter to academic achievement, with the important caveat that whether it matters depends upon how it is used".

In another recent study undertaken by the Bertelsmann Foundation of students in a German school and a school in the United States concluded "that the use of media and technology improves learning outcomes, instills key qualifications for the information age, and increases motivation". And finally, one concern often expressed about ICT is that its use will isolate students from each other and from their teachers. In a 10-year longitudinal study undertaken by Apple Computer, "Dispelling widespread myths, the researchers found that instead of isolating students, access to technology actually encouraged them to collaborate more than in traditional classrooms. And instead of becoming boring with use, technology was even more interesting to students as they began using it for creating and communicating". It appears, therefore, that ICT, properly used, may enhance and increase communications between people.

In conclusion, evidence has consistently shown ICT-mediated instruction using conventional teaching methods is as good as traditional face-to-face instruction and, in the case of computer-based instruction, may in select instances improve student learning and attitudes towards learning. However, the picture is less clear - but promising - for more sophisticated uses of ICT in the classroom, especially for the host of applications and methods that support "constructivist" learning, in which students are encouraged to work in rich environments of information and experience to build their own understandings about them. Worldwide, research into the effectiveness of ICT-mediated instruction is continuing and should provide a clearer picture of the effectiveness of ICT in supporting constructivist pedagogy.

ICT-enabled education

A second way to assess the merit of ITC-use in education

is to consider what, if anything, such use enables students and teachers to do that they would not otherwise be able to do. To explore this question, we consider five aspects of the educational use of ICT -supporting new pedagogical methods, accessing remote resources, enabling collaboration, extending educational programs, and developing skills for the workplace.

Modern constructivist educational theory emphasizes critical thinking, problem solving, 'authentic' learning experiences, social negotiation of knowledge, and collaboration -pedagogical methods that change the role of the teacher from disseminator of information to learning facilitator, helping students as they actively engage with information and materials to construct their own understandings. That is, students learn how to learn, not just what to learn. ICT has the potential to be used in support of these new educational methods, as tools enabling students' learning by doing. ICT can make it possible for teachers to engage students in self-paced, self-directed problem-based or constructivist learning experiences; and also test student learning in new, interactive, and engaging ways that may better assess deep understanding of content and processes. Two examples may help illustrate how ICT can support constructivist teaching methods. Computer Supported Intentional Learning Environments (CSILE), developed at the Ontario Institute for Studies in Education, is a network system that provides support for collaborative learning and inquiry within a school. CSILE promotes student interaction through referencing, connecting ideas, sharing authorship, and "building-on" the work of others to advance knowledge.

The central feature of CSILE is a 'communal' database into which students can enter text and graphics, and can read, add to, and comment on other's work. The commercial version of CSILE, Knowledge Base, is being used in both work and educational settings in Canada, Japan, the United States, Finland, and the Netherlands. The Physics Teaching Studio, pioneered at the Rensselaer Polytechnic Institute in the United States, incorporates the systematic use of ICT in a cooperative learning environment for instruction in undergraduate physics. Laboratory data acquisition and analysis tools are embedded into a hypermedia text that introduces scientific topics, links the students to related materials, and poses questions for the students to answer with the ICT tools. Studio courses emphasize a hands-on, learning by doing approach engaging students in various problem solving and active learning sessions. This approach has been applied to mathematics courses and the concept has spread to other universities including City University of Hong Kong and Curtin University of Technology in Australia.

Improved assessment tools can also be developed using ICT. Such assessments can engage students in tasks that require data manipulation, simulation or other interactive acts of knowledge construction. VizQuiz is a multimedia program that allows students to take a chemistry quiz at a computer, but with the added advantage that color graphics, animations, and video clips can be included in the questions. In addition to multimedia capability, such programs can provide hints, remedial feedback, worked out solutions or explanations, and instantaneous grading. However, although ICT offers the opportunity to construct powerful learning experiences, it is pedagogically neutral. That is, instead of being used in the ways described above, ICT can be used in support of traditional teaching methodologies like the large group lecture, student note taking, and examinations. Teachers can use a computer and projector to show slides to illustrate a lecture, students can use laptop computers to take notes during the lecture, and multiple choice quizzes about the content of the lecture can be put on a website. How these new ICT tools and resources will be used is a human decision, not inherent in the technologies themselves.

As previously mentioned, connectivity is one of the main differences between older and new ICTs. Below, we discuss two aspects of connectivity—access to material and to human resources. Historically, information resources at libraries, schools, and universities have only been available within the walls of these institutions, in a wide variety of physical media, at certain times of the day, and in limited quantities. Because of advances in ICT, it is no longer necessary for students and teachers to be at a certain location at a specific time to acquire a physical object. The Internet represents the greatest collection of human knowledge ever assembled, and it is available to every student and teacher properly equipped with ICT. An unlimited number of digital representations of physical objects can now be made available to students at any time and from any place. Digital library initiatives are being undertaken in countries around the world that will provide collections that are electronically accessible of the Internet including printed works (e.g., textbooks, journals, illustrations, maps, charts and graphs), photographs, films and videotapes, paintings, 3D models, graphics, animations, software, reference materials, audio files, and so forth. A joint effort between the European Union and the National Science Foundation in the United States is exploring international collaboration on research to develop such libraries. Specialized collections of digital information are also being created. For example, the entire works of William Shakespeare may be accessed, searched, and downloaded from a website at the Massachusetts Institute of Technology (MIT).

Web-based language dictionaries, such as the LEO English/German Dictionary, provide a means to translate words and phrases from one language to another. A virtual tour and access to digitized images of major works from its collection. The NASA Image eXchange offers access to hundreds of thousands of images taken by US spacecraft of the Earth, the planets, moons, asteroids, and other extra-terrestrial bodies. Thousands of websites now exist that contain collections of high quality curriculum guides, lesson plans, and instructional activities. For example, the United Nations CyberSchoolBus website contains teaching units on urbanization, disease, the environment, and women and politics, as well as interactive games, maps, databases, and quizzes. Specialized websites designed to provide information and assistance in specific subject areas are also proliferating. Lingu@NET is a website developed by the British government to provide "quality-assured resources for language teachers and learners worldwide".

And finally, remote access to expensive scientific instrumentation is also possible. In the United Kingdom, the Virtual Microscope of the Open University can be used by students to view slides over the Internet (or from a CD-ROM version). The Hands-On Universe, at the Lawrence Berkeley National Laboratory, co-funded by several U.S. government agencies, has developed and piloted an educational program that enables high school students to request their own observations from telescopes at professional observatories. Students download digital images to their classroom computers and use powerful image processing software to visualize and analyze their data. This ability to access remote resources and use them locally, although not without negative aspects, fundamentally changes the quantity, nature, and potential uses of information resources available for educational purposes. In addition to efforts to digitize existing physical resources, many new information resources (e.g., websites, digital images, electronic journals and newsletters) are being created which can only be accessed electronically. As digital representations of physical resources are created, and as more information resources are distributed only in digital format, it will be critical that students and teachers have ICT access.

ICT enables educational collaborations between individuals and groups of people. Such collaborations may take place locally or between people in widely separated geographical locations. They may be temporary or long-term. Students?12 may collaborate with peers in other schools, teachers may collaborate with university professors, members of the local business community may serve as mentors to students, scientists in government agencies may work with school children, and so forth. Only educational usefulness and access to ICT limit the possibilities. Email, computer-mediated conferencing, and desktop videoconferencing are all being used to support collaboration between individuals and groups. Collaborations are also taking place by means of real-time chat systems; whiteboards; newsgroups; computer-mediated conferencing (CMC); and specialized software like CaMILE: Collaborative and Multimedia Interactive Learning Environment and The Knowledge Integration Environment. Other applications include MUDs (Multi-User Domains) MOOs (Multi-user domain, Object Oriented), and MUSHs (Multi-User Shared

Hallucinations). Such applications are Internet-accessible, text-mediated virtual environments in which participants can both interact with others as well as help construct the common virtual space. At the University of California, Berkeley, classes in language, literature, linguistics, law, and communications are making use of such applications. Combinations of these ICT applications are also frequently used in educational programs.

Online experts

Many organizations offer 'ask an expert' services. For example, students may send inquiries about scientific topics to working scientists at the Canadian Centre for Marine Geology of Dalhousie University and the US Argonne National Laboratory. In other examples, online experts offer advice in health, weather topics, and construction engineering. In an extreme example of how ICT can bridge distance to enable students to access remote expertise, last spring students from four universities in the US and Canada and discussed physiology experiments with astronauts orbiting the Earth aboard the space shuttle Columbia.

ICT can also enable mentoring programs to provide one-on-one guidance to individuals by well-established members of a particular community. Such virtual collaborations between individuals are an effective ways for senior members of a community to teach, inspire, and support newcomers. Mentor High School in the United States offers an electronic Quest Forum in which freshmen students may discuss course options with students in the senior class.

Virtual learning communities

ICT makes it possible to engage people in widely dispersed locations in 'virtual learning communities.' Virtual learning communities are learning groups based on shared purpose, not artificial distinctions of location or age. Through ICT, learners can be drawn together from almost anywhere, and they can construct their own formal or informal learning groups. Such communities may transverse barriers of time, geography, age, ability, culture, and social status. ICT that supports such efforts can be as simple as email or as sophisticated as desktop videoconferencing systems. In an example of how email is being used to enable virtual learning communities, a course titled International E-Mail Debate is being offered by professors at universities in Turkey, the United States, Germany, and the Czech Republic to promote writing skills across cultures and enhance intercultural awareness. Students enrolled in the course debate position papers on timely and relevant topics using E-mail.

Virtual Design Studios, begun in 1993, are collaborations between teams of Architecture students in universities worldwide. Teachers and students, on different continents and in different time zones, work on a common design, using computer-aided design systems, email, a central database, and video-conferencing. Participants use the World Wide Web to display their designs and a virtual international jury of architects and teachers judges the relative merit of the work. Past student included re-designing housing in Shanghai and designing a Center for Cultural and Religious Studies in Japan. A similar effort took place in 1996 between students and teachers at Union College (USA), METU (Turkey), and Queen's University (Canada). Virtual Design Studio techniques are being utilized by other disciplines, such as Engineering. The Global Learning and Observations to Benefit the Environment (Globe) program, sponsored by the U.S. Government, links students, teachers, and the scientific research community worldwide in a virtual learning community to study the global environment. Internationally, GLOBE is being implemented through bilateral agreements between the U.S. government and governments of partner nations. As of December 1998, thousands of schools in 74 countries have registered as participants. In the GLOBE program, scientists design protocols for specific measurements they need for Earth Science research that can be performed by K-12 students. Teachers are trained in the GLOBE protocols and teach them to their students. Students make the measurements, enter data via the Internet to a central data archive, and the data becomes available to scientists and the general community. Scientific visualizations of the data are provided over the Internet. Students benefit by having a 'hands-on' experience in science, math, and technology, using their own local environment as a learning laboratory. Students also benefit from the opportunity to communicate with their peers around the world, thus increasing not only their environmental understanding but also their understanding of other cultures and their sense of global community.

Beginning in 1995, a series of online 'Quest' have brought together students and teachers together around the world into a virtual community to learn about specific topics framed in an interactive learning expedition. For example, during MayaQuest, a 1995-96, over one million students, teachers, and others from around the globe followed the progress of a five-rider scientific bike expedition among Mayan ruins in Mexico and Central

America, learning about the ancient Mayan civilization and learning from on-site archaeologists. The bicyclists carried laptop computers and a satellite dish to connect to the Internet. Students voted on team decisions, explored 21 Maya sites and were virtually on hand for several major archaeological discoveries. The original MayaQuest website (no longer available) received over a 1.2 million hits in 90 days. It offered team updates, photographs, teachers' guides, and direct interaction with eight of the world's top archaeologists. The company has since offered educational scientific expeditions to Africa and the Galapagos Islands. Other organizations are offering online learning adventures for teachers and students.

Using specialized software, teachers can create Internet-based simulations for role-playing activities in language learning. The simulations, incorporating email, chat, and online creation and editing of documents, are thought to motivate oral and written communication amongst the participating groups, while students are guided through scenarios relevant to the country of their chosen language. The UNICEF Voices of Youth website offers opportunities for teachers and students to participate in discussions on current global issues, such as the effects of war on children; take part in interactive global learning, and exchange experiences about the use ICT in education.

Home/school communications

Although such virtual learning communities can span the globe, they can also be formed locally. For example, in the U.S., students, parents, teachers, and administrators in the Los Angeles Unified School District's, REBUILD have joined together into a virtual learning community with the objective of improving the performance of Limited English Proficient (LEP) students. Staff at 11 schools are using interactive videoconferencing over computer networks to jointly plan lessons and team-teach from different sites. All students in REBUILD schools, mostly minority children, are provided with access to the Internet and electronic mail in their classrooms and from their homes. Homework assignments are placed on the web and informal parent-teacher conferences take place electronically whenever necessary. Staff members at the school sites receive continuing professional development instruction and consultation via videoconferencing from staff at the Center for Language Minority Education and Research at California State University Long Beach.

Students in the program have made substantial gains in English reading proficiency. In the United Kingdom, Microsoft, Comtel and International Computers Limited (ICL) have funded the Highdown Information Hub which connects homes and schools via the Internet. Parents are able to send email to their children at school during the working day, view that their children are working on, and electronically converse with teachers, opening up new learning opportunities by enabling close collaboration between parents, students, and teachers.

ICT makes it possible to extend the reach of educational programs in two important ways. First, ICT makes it possible to deliver educational programs anywhere in the world. Second, ICT also can help individuals learn throughout their lifetime.

Distance (distributed) education

Distance education programs, also known as 'distributed'

education programs, are those in which the teacher and students are physically separated, and teaching and learning takes place by means of single technologies or combinations of ICTs. In the past, such programs made use of print, radio, and television. Now, new ICTs are driving changes in these traditional 'open' or distance education programs. Such programs are increasing using the Internet and the World Wide Web for the delivery of courses. For example, the International Francophone Consortium of Distance and Open Learning Institutions (CIFFAD), a consortium of open and distance learning institutions spread over 49 countries, of which 80% are in developing nations, has recently entered into a phase of reengineering to make use of new ICTs. The group aims to provide at least one hundred access points to the Internet per year in member establishments with the major part of the consortium having access to the network by the end of 1998. In an initiative making use of a combination of virtual and traditional educational programs, Singapore's two leading research universities - the National University of Singapore and Nanyang Technological University - and The Massachusetts Institute of Technology in the U.S. recently signed an agreement to "create a new global model for long-distance engineering education and research".

The jointly developed degree programs will enroll their first students in July 1999, and will be created and delivered by instructors from the three institutions, using a combination of faculty and student exchanges and state-of-the-art communications technology. Typically, distance education courses have been offered as supplementary programs by campus-based educational institutions. Now, however, digital ICTs have stimulated the creation of "virtual" non-profit and for-profit educational institutions that exist partially or only in "cyberspace" and whose programs are offered entirely by means of ICT. Such efforts are making it possible for ICT-equipped individuals located anywhere to participate in educational programs. The Western Governors University is an example of a "virtual university," a university that has no physical campus. WGU, initiated in 1996 by the governors of 18 of the Western United States, is a competency-based, degree-granting, virtual university: "a 'cyber' university that is not bound by its location because it doesn't have a campus in the physical sense. The Open University in the United Kingdom and the Virtual University of the Monterrey Institute of Technology in Mexico to collaborate on the development and delivery of distance learning programs.

In Germany, the four Baden universities Freiburg, Karlsruhe, Mannheim and Heidelberg recently announced the establishment of that country's first virtual university. The initiative's objective is to establish individual distance learning via e-mail, ISDN or digital television. In Africa, the World Bank is funding the development of the African Virtual University (AVU). This effort holds great promise for improving educational access for people on a continent where relatively few enjoy the benefits of education, let alone a tertiary education:

> Very few African countries have attained primary education for all, despite the fact that many have been independent for some thirty years. At secondary level, the record is even worse, with many African countries able to provide secondary education to only 4 or 5 per cent of the age-group. Most African countries can boast of less than one per cent of the relevant age-group attaining any form of tertiary education, compared to between 25 per cent

> and 75 per cent in industrialized countries. And those who do attain tertiary education are unlikely to specialize in science or technology.

AVU completed a pilot phase in 1996-98 and is now moving into an operational phase when it will begin delivering full-fledged undergraduate degree programs in Science and Engineering in January1999. The AVU's programs will be delivered by a combination of ICT including interactive television and the Internet. The program is developing a digital library of scientific engineering as a resource to students and teachers. Virtual educational programs are not limited to postsecondary education. The U.S. Department of Education has funded the Virtual High School (VHS), a collaborative of U.S. high schools that develops and shares web-based courses.

During the 1997-98 school year, VHS offered 29 Internet-based, credit-bearing courses to about 500 students in 27 schools located in 10 states. This approach is thought to be particularly useful as many of the participating schools either have no qualified teacher or insufficient enrollment to justify individually offering some of the courses available through the collaborative. In addition to traditional institutions using ICT to enhance or create distance learning programs, commercial companies like Sylvan Learning Systems, Inc, in the United States and the Wall Street Institute School of English in Europe are starting ICT-based for-profit distance education programs. Although alternate and distance education providers currently make up less than 2% of the postsecondary education market, almost $2 billion dollars has been raised on Wall Street since 1996 to finance such new ventures.

Unlike in the past when a person's education took place for a specific period of time during their youth, education is now widely seen as a continuing activity taking place throughout the lifespan. Establishing lifelong learning habits among citizens and providing lifelong learning opportunities has become a major goal of government initiatives worldwide. Lifelong learning is thought to be important for at least two reasons. First, it is no longer possible to master an entire discipline in a few short years. The amount of information available and the speed at which new information is being created makes this impossible. Consider, for example, that printed scientific information doubles approximately every 10 years. Half of all available scientific information has been published in the last 10 years. Second, career changes are becoming more frequent as are changing requirements within individual professions. For example, the People's Republic of China is facing changes of unprecedented magnitude in its traditional industries, and a large number of workers are being forced to change careers or take early retirement.

In order for these industries to survive and to take advantage of market opportunities, the workforce will need to be upgraded to work at higher knowledge levels with new technology. Because ICT can enable teaching and learning from anywhere at anytime, it is seen as an effective means to provide lifelong educational opportunities. The World Bank's Consultative Group on International Agricultural Research (CGIAR) noted:

> In industrialized nations, it is widely recognized that lifelong learning has become essential in a world driven by new science and technologies, with frequent retraining being needed for many

> professions. Fortunately, we now have a new tool that makes this type of education much more readily possible. The Worldwide Web is being used as a direct teaching tool that allows virtual classrooms of interacting students and faculty to be created through "asynchronous learning networks."

Many examples of how ICT is being used to foster and encourage lifelong learning can be found. In Africa, LWF is supporting the implementation of "Multipurpose Community Telecenters" in five countries at which locals may have affordable access to ICT. By enabling users to share the costs of facilities and support, the Telecentres will offer low-cost means of Internet access as well as information support for literacy campaigns, basic and non-formal education, and information on government programs. The Telecenters will also provide facilities for the generation and exchange of community-based information. In Great Britain, the Department for Education and Employment has established a 'UK Lifelong Learning' website that provides news and lists of lifelong learning opportunities. Earlier this year, the Dutch government launched a national program for lifelong learning "to ensure that better use is made of the country's intellectual resources." As part of the program, teacher-training colleges will receive extra funding to experiment with ICT. The European Lifelong Learning Initiative makes use of ICT, "to initiate the dissemination of information, the co-ordination of projects and studies, the mobilisation of actions, people and organisations to bring Europe into the Lifelong Learning Age. It covers all sectors and all countries".

The Asia Pacific Economic Cooperation (APEC) Forum has established three mechanisms to assist countries across the area to establish lifelong learning: the creation of a database of Asian scholars, researchers and practitioners involved with lifelong learning issues and programming across the region; the development and publication of a book of papers on lifelong learning policies, practices and programs across the Asia Pacific region; and a lifelong learning conference for APEC members to discuss issues identified in the book.

After leaving school to embark on a career, young people can expect the day-to-day practice of every discipline to be affected by the use of ICT. In the future, economic competitiveness, employment, and personal fulfillment may no longer be based on the production of physical goods. Personal and national wealth creation may be linked to the production and dissemination of knowledge and depend on research, education and training, and on the capacity to innovate. Having advanced ICT skills and knowing how to use discipline-specific applications may help students secure suitable employment and enhance their productivity once employed. Furthermore, as has been noted above, the ability to engage in life-long learning opportunities offered by educational institutions around the world is increasingly dependent upon access to, and use of, ICT. In light of changing perceptions about what constitutes appropriate skills for the modern era, some organizations are promulgating educational standards, attempting to codify what all students should learn about ICT. For example, the National Educational Technology Standards (NETS) in the United States has released an initial set of national educational technology standards for pre-college students (cnets.iste.org). The NET standards are divided into six categories including "Basic Operations and Concepts," "Social, Ethical, and Human Issues," "Technology Productivity Tools," "Technology

Communications Tools," "Technology Research Tools," and "Technology Problem-Solving and Decision-Making Tools".

However, although it can be anticipated that the increasing use of ICT in education and society will change the nature of the knowledge and skills students must acquire in order to compete and contribute in an increasingly ICT-dominated global economy, what skills will be necessary is not clear:

> What do students need to know and do with technology? Unlike the more stable content and goals we have for other areas of school study, technology continues to change and evolve; with these changes come ever-new goals for how technology should serve learning, and what students should know about technology. A review of the "prevailing wisdom" about appropriate technology use since the early 1980s takes one down an ever-turning road that includes programming in BASIC, then with LOGO; and on to drill and practice applications on integrated systems; word-processing and curriculum-specific tools like history databases, simulations, and microcomputer-based labs; then multimedia; the Internet; and now Web page design. While there may be some logic to this progression, the reality is that, just as educators get their arms around one approach, with the attendant investments in software, training and possible curricular readjustments, the messages about appropriate technology use change.

There does seem to be a growing consensus that all students must achieve "Information literacy": "It is the task of general education to provide every girl and boy with the versatile basic skills in acquiring, managing and communicating information which are necessary in the information society and essential for successful further study". The American Library Association has outlined seven steps representing the basic elements in an information literacy curriculum: Defining the need for information, initiating the search strategy, locating the resources, assessing and comprehending the information, interpreting the information, communication the information, and evaluating the product and process. Genric skills that "information society literate" citizens should have, suggest three categories into which such skills might be categorized: Connectivity, Logic, and the Structuring of Data and Information. It is clear that new skills and knowledge will be necessary to compete and contribute in a global "knowledge society." However, because of the rapid pace of change of ICTs, it is less clear what skills can be taught to today's students that will still be relevant by the time they graduate and enter the workforce. Focusing on concepts like "information literacy," rather than on specific technologies or applications, may be essential in planning and developing new curricula.

The third issue we consider when assessing the effectiveness of ICT in education is the question of cost-effectiveness - information is of critical importance, especially to developing countries with fewer resources to invest. However, assessing the cost-effectiveness of ICT in education is difficult, if not impossible, for at least four reasons -lack of meaningful data, variability in the implementation of ICTs, difficulty of generalizing from specific programs, and difficulty of assessing the value of qualitative educational differences. In addition, cost-analyses do not consider the societal and economic consequences of not investing in ICT for education. First, direct comparisons between traditional and ICT-based educational programs are hard to make because meaningful data are lacking. When considering the costs associated with ICT use, what variables are included in such studies vary widely. For example, in addition to hardware and software costs such an analysis may or may not take into account factors such as teacher training, support personnel, facilities renovation, security systems, insurance, and so forth. Furthermore, many institutions making use of ICT in their programs simply do not collect such data. Problems in conducting a cost-analysis in developing countries because of the lack of local effective efforts to do real world cost analysis and the difficulty to obtain the kind of information we would have liked to include in our cost analyses.

Second, there is the question of which technologies and applications to compare. The costs associated with any ICT-based educational program may merely indicate the choices that have been made, not the choices that are possible. Evaluating the cost-effectiveness of email-based courses will return a different result than comparing courses using videoconferencing technologies, although the educational goals may be similar. Making judgments as to the cost-effectiveness of ICT-use in general from the analysis of particular programs is difficult. Third, as has been noted earlier, ICTs are not single technologies or applications, but an array of possibilities. Many ICT-based educational programs use a combination of technologies and applications, making the analysis of costs and comparisons with other programs even more difficult. This is further complicated because of the rapid evolution of ICT and changes in its uses in education. Studies typically take a long time to complete and longitudinal studies take years. Such efforts may be doomed to failure because the subject under study is a moving target.

And finally, there is the question of what metrics are useful in measuring "effectiveness." Is "effectiveness" determined by units of instructional time, by student retention rates, by performance on assessments? Quantitative measures are easier to construct but may not ultimately tell us much. Qualitative differences may ultimately be more important in assessing the cost-effectiveness of ICT, but may not be measurable. For example, approaches to incorporating ICT into education can be roughly grouped into three categories - learning about (computer literacy and programming), learning by (drill and practice and tutorial software), and learning with computers (collaborating with remote groups, conducting research over the Internet).

None-the-less, even in the face of such obstacles, attempts to establish the relative costs of ICTs in education. In general, these studies find that the use of new ICTs is more expensive that instruction delivered by older technologies like print and radio, but less expensive than instruction delivered by television.

Education and ICT in Latin America and the Caribbean, the costs of using a computer with an Internet connection in a school was much less expensive per pupil than broadcast television, but substantially more expensive than radio. It should be noted that even these findings may be misleading because of the variability across regions and individual countries in the cost of Internet access and what such costs mean in the real income of individuals in various countries. As should be clear from the information below, although Internet access is absolutely less expensive in Africa than Europe, the "real" cost to individual users in Africa is much higher. Currently, the average cost of using the Internet for 5 hours a month in Africa is about $60/month. This contrasts with figures of the Organization for Economic Cooperation and Development (OECD) which estimated recently that 20 hours of Internet access in the U.S. costs $29, including phone and provider fees. Although European charges are more all of these countries have per capita incomes which are 10 - 100 times greater than the African average. Despite the general lack of cost data that can be used to estimate the cost of information technology in developing countries, compare the per pupil costs of setting up a computer laboratory in a school for computer-assisted instruction. A similar analysis of the costs of equipping a classroom, not a laboratory.

ICT in developing countries, assessed the annual per-student cost of providing computers for instruction in developing countries at $84 USD. This finding is in close agreement with the study by Potashnik and Adkins. By extrapolating the expenses if 30 computers were used 300 days per year, 10 hours per day, as a resource to raise the skills and education levels of all members of the community, not just students, Osin estimates the cost drops to 34 cents per hour of interaction. He concludes, "There is no alternative system known that may provide the benefits possible by integrating computers in the education system, while at the same time serving the whole community."

Another factor that must be considered when calculating the cost-effectiveness of ICT use is the question of alternatives. The costs of building sufficient campuses to handle the rising demand for education may be prohibitive. Virtual educational institutions do not require the same campus infrastructure and related costs traditional campus-based institutions must support.

The number of places in conventional colleges and universities and school systems will always be limited, reflecting in part the fixed capacities of the campus and the faculty. Developmental and operational costs associated with conventional colleges and universities are high. By comparison, distance education has lower start-up costs, and much lower operational costs. With 'campus-free" distance education, variable costs, once the system is operational, tend to be flat. That is, beyond a relatively small number of students, the costs per student are the same or slightly less. The increasing use of technology to broaden the scope of distance education has great potential for further reducing costs per student. In Chinese Taipei, the distance education-based National Open University, with its budget of NT$800,000,000, accommodates approximately 30,000 adult students each year. By comparison, the National Taiwan University, one of the larger universities in Chinese Taipei, has an annual budget of $NT3,500,000,000 for its 21,000 students. Though gross numbers of this sort beg some level of refinement, the differential costs remain substantial and manifest.

The above analysis does not consider that other costs, such as curriculum development and library resources, can be shared across virtual collaborations of institutions thereby lowering the costs to individual institutions. For example, the Pennsylvania Online World of Electronic Resources (Library POWER) initiative, will make thousands of periodicals and documents accessible over the Internet to state residents.

And finally, when discussing cost-effectiveness, one must consider the societal costs to developing countries of not preparing their citizens to participate in an information-based global society. The World Development

Bank warns that the global explosion of knowledge may either lift hundreds of millions of the world's poor out of poverty or it may create a widening knowledge gap, in which poor countries lag further and further behind:

> If knowledge gaps widen, the world will be split further, not just by disparities in capital and other resources, but by the disparity of knowledge. Increasingly, capital and other resources will flow to those countries with the stronger knowledge bases, reinforcing inequality.

The ICT can play a major role to play in reducing information inequities:

> This new technology greatly facilitates the acquisition and absorption of knowledge, offering developing countries unprecedented opportunities to enhance educational systems, improve policy formation and execution, and widen the range of opportunities for business and the poor. One of the greatest hardships endured by the poor, and by many others who live in the poorest countries, is their sense of isolation. The new communications technologies promise to reduce that sense of isolation, and to open access to knowledge in ways unimaginable not long ago. And, as Potashnik and Adkins have pointed out, "even in countries which do not believe in the cost-effectiveness of information technology as a tool for mass education, it is important that they begin acquiring experience using this technology for educational purposes. Otherwise, educators in developing countries will be marginalized in the international dialogue on education".

In conclusion, assessing the effectiveness of ICT in education is a difficulty, multidimensional endeavor. When comparing ICT-mediated instruction with face-to-face instruction, it seems clear that ICT-mediated instruction is at least as effective. When considering what ICT-use enables educationally, it seems equally clear that ICT-enabled education has a distinct advantage over traditional methods in its ability to support new pedagogical methods, provide access to remote resources, enable collaboration, reach more people less expensively, and reach them throughout their lifespan. When considering whether ICT is "cost-effective" in educational settings, a definitive conclusion may not be possible for a variety of reasons. However, when considering the alternative of building more physical infrastructure, the cost savings to be realized from sharing resources, and the societal price of not providing access, ICT as a means of enabling teaching and learning appears to be an attractive and necessary alternative.

Creating an ICT-Enabled Learning Environment

In this section, we will concentrate on the development of ICT-enabled learning environments, specifically on infrastructure, content, teacher education and training, and technical support.

In order to make use of digital ICTs schools must be equipped with computers. In order to access the Internet from a computer, schools, homes, libraries, and other educational venues must be equipped with an Internet connection, either by means of the telephone or cable network and a modem or a direct connection. Many creative means to providing computers and building the necessary Internet infrastructure are being explored in countries throughout the world.

Collaboration, including cost sharing, between education and industry to build ICT infrastructure is becoming commonplace.

One promising approach to equipping schools with computers inexpensively is to transfer the technology from government organizations and businesses to schools. In the U.S., the Government's Computers for Learning program donates surplus federal computer equipment to schools and non-profit educational organizations. Established by Executive Order, the program aims to provide hundreds of thousands of computers for teaching and learning. Other non-governmental programs, such as the non-profit Detwiler Foundation's Computers for Schools and the charitable organization Computers for Children in the United States and the industry supported Computers for Schools program in Canada, are soliciting donations of "obsolete" or redundant computers from business, industry, and individuals, and refurbishing them before donating them to schools. The goal of the Computers for Schools program in Canada is to place 250,000 computers in schools and public libraries by 2001. To date, the program has donated over 70,000 refurbished computers to Canadian schools and libraries.

Although not primarily intended as infrastructure, partnerships between schools and universities often result in new infrastructure development. These typically target university/school connectivity for research, teacher education, and Internet access.

'Netday' initiatives, characterized as 'high-tech barn-raising,' are grass-roots efforts by community volunteers to wire classrooms, libraries, and computer labs so that they may connect to the Internet. Organizers of such efforts typically help schools to develop a technical plan that includes instructional goals, network and wiring architecture, network management and technical support, training, and an operating budget. On a specific day, volunteers from the local community do the physical labor necessary to run network wiring; greatly reducing the costs of providing Internet access within the schools.

Netdays began in 1995 as a local initiative in California, but have since become an annual national initiative endorsed by the President of the United States, and have spread to countries throughout the world. For example, Netdays now take place Australia, many European countries.

Although not strictly intended for educational purposes, many Community Networking initiatives have educational components and are worthy of mention. Community networks bring together entire villages, towns or cities into virtual communities to strengthening social ties, promote social participation, promote economic development, and build a sense of civic responsibility. Such initiatives establish affordable, community operated ICT systems that involve local individuals and organizations in learning about electronic communications, and help construct these systems to meet unique local needs.

In an interesting example of how community networking can benefit educational institutions, the International Telecomputing Consortium is working with schools and universities in China to create school-based community networks. In these participating schools establish computer centers with Internet access for use by students and teachers in class. After hours, the center is open to parents and other members of the community who may not have Internet access. Teachers and students in these schools provide ICT training for members of the community. The school thus becomes the Internet access point for the entire community with some revenue going back to the school. Another useful method of providing support for ICT in education is the provision of specialized grants to individuals and educational institutions. Such grants programs serve a dual purpose of stimulating innovation in the educational community and targeting scarce resources on particularly promising applications.

Many for-profit and non-profit organizations offer such grants to teachers and schools. For example, the Hewlett-Packard, Compaq, IBM, and Microsoft companies all offer equipment grants to educators. In the United States, the Department of Education's Technology Innovation Challenge Grants annually funds large-scale educational innovations with ICT.

Beyond equipment and software, appropriate content is necessary to make use of ICT for educational purposes. In this section, we consider a few of the many initiatives related to educational content creation and standards.

Content is being created by many organizations including governmental agencies, commercial and non-profit organizations, mainstream and extremist political and religious groups, social clubs, universities, colleges, trade unions, public and private schools, libraries; collaborations between such groups; and individuals. Although some online content is specifically designed for educational purposes, most is not. Indeed, the sheer amount of information available on the Internet, the ease with which it may be accessed, and the lack of standards for cataloging such information have created problems of information overload and quality control for parents, students, and educators worldwide. These problems, coupled with the preponderance of Internet-accessible content having been produced by a few developed countries - particularly the United States have led many to believe the Internet is a mixed blessing for education. The speed of the development of information overload may be illustrated by the fact that in June 1993 there were only 130 websites worldwide. By January 1997 this number had grown to a staggering 650,000. The number of websites has been more than doubling, sometimes trebling, every year since 1993 and is expected to do so for the foreseeable future. As each website usually contains multiple webpages, it is literally impossible for one person to view every webpage on the Internet. In another example, it is estimated that there were fewer than 100 Chinese webpages in 1994. Today, estimates place the number at over a quarter million offering everything from book reviews to travel guides, and the numbers continue to increase dramatically.

Countries with similar languages, cultures, or that have migrant populations may be able to economize in the creation of ICT-based content and tools by collaboration. For example, in Europe, the TOPILOT telematics involved a management team and 15 school-based partners in the UK, the Netherlands, Belgium, and Germany in the development of a multimedia educational program for fairground, circus, and bargee families within the European Community, all living a traveling life-style. The developed interactive CD-ROMs students could use while on the road as well as tools to be used for Internet-based interaction between tutors and students.

One approach to facilitating access to appropriate educational content is the creation of a 'Schoolnet.' Schoolnets, also known as 'national education grids,' are regional, national or local projects that may include efforts to physically wire schools to information services, but that are fundamentally developed to provide access to appropriate educational content. Schoolnets may contain curriculum guides; collaborative online projects; email directories; links to other teachers, schools, and governmental organizations; online classes; tutorials; and news about conferences. For example, the United Kingdom's National Grid for Learning (NGfL) "is both an architecture (or structure) of educationally valuable content on the Internet, and a programme for developing the means to access that content in schools, libraries, colleges, universities, workplaces, homes and elsewhere". Schoolnet are being developed worldwide. European Schoolnet, of the European Union, offers teachers access to a wealth of information about ICT use in education. Schoolnets now exist in Canada, France, Ireland, Japan, South Africa, Thailand, and other countries.

The Canadian government has recently signed an agreement with the China State Education Commission and a Sino-Canadian joint business venture to establish a Sino-Canada SchoolNet that will develop online Chinese-Canadian educational programs and resources. This will deliver services to students and teachers in both countries through a virtual campus. One of the advantages of new ICTs is that it empowers users to not only consume information, but also produce it. With a computer, printer, and desktop publishing software, any local educational group can produce high quality printed materials. With an Internet connection and website, any educational organization can "publish" content derived from local knowledge and experiences. For example, eighth grade students in the United States at Dakota Meadows Middle School in North Mankato, Minnesota, have written short, two-minute mysteries posting them on the World Wide Web and challenging other students to "Use your wits and detective skills to solve these cases." Over 20,000 people have visited the students' website. These same students have collected oral histories from members of the Mankato community about their experiences during World War II and made them available on the web. In another example, the Summer Institute of Linguistics (SIL) has helped set-up Literacy and Awareness Publication (LAMP) centers in each of the 20 provinces of Papua New Guinea to promote literacy in approximately 850 local languages. Few, if any, literacy materials exist in the majority of these languages, and over 55 per cent of the population aged over 10 is functionally illiterate. At these centers, literacy texts are produced covering a wide variety of subjects including healthcare, hygiene and preservation of the environment that can be shared between the centers. The computers, scanners, digital duplicators might be new technology, but the materials produced on this equipment are in local languages based on local customs and culture for local audiences.

At the moment, finding specific educational materials on the World Wide Web can be likened to a difficult and cumbersome scavenger hunt, often resulting in wasted time and unexpected results. For example, a teacher searching the Web using a popular search engine, Alta Vista, for educational materials on "Southeast Asia" would find over 77,000 related webpages including information about books, travel agencies, journals, music, colleges, personal travelogues, pictures, satellite images, maps, newspaper articles, and so forth. On the other hand, if the teacher had entered "Asia, Southeast", the search would return over 800,000 webpages! Faced with such a hodgepodge of information, a teacher or student is hard-pressed to locate specific information or materials of use within the curriculum at a particular grade level. The results of such indiscriminate searches also raise the issue of the validity and reliability of the information.

Once found, because of varying technical standards, materials created with one ICT-based learning system may not be usable in a different environment. Several efforts to bring order to the chaos of the Internet and World Wide Web are underway.

By the creation of technical standards, like the Dublin Core Metadata Initiative and the Instructional Management Systems (IMS) may 'help transform the end-user experience of the Web from the unstructured tangle it is today into something more like a digital library or virtual learning centre'. If international agreement can be reached on an acceptable set of technical standards, educational materials developers will be able to embed in electronic materials information such as subject matter, grade level, educational objectives, and pedagogical approach. Teachers and students will then be able to search for educational materials with common descriptors and be assured that the materials, once found, will be compatible with local ICT applications.

Teacher education and training

To create ICT-enabled teaching and learning environments, it is also necessary to provide ICT training for teachers. The changes being asked of faculty members in restructuring their work lives will be extraordinary and will require them to function in ways they never conceived of and for which they were not trained." In some countries, for example Great Britain, it is now required to have training in ICT-use to earn a teaching credential. Beyond preparative training, as educational applications of ICT continue to evolve, refresher training for experienced teachers will be necessary. In one possible framework for organizing ICT training for teachers, McDougall and Squires identify five foci: (1) skills with particular applications, (2) integration into existing curricula, (3) IT related changes in curricula, (4) changes in teacher role, and (5) underpinning theories of education.

But, even more vital than ICT training for teachers and administrators, there is a continuing need to educate qualified teachers to staff schools. ICT is being used in a wide variety of ways to support teacher education as well and teacher training in ICT use. Email, websites, desktop videoconferencing, and other technologies and applications are all playing a role in such efforts.

Teacher education

Preservice teacher education refers to the formal preparation of individuals to enter the classroom as qualified teachers. Inservice teacher education refers to on-going professional development programs offered to teachers once they have entered the profession. In a review of ICT use in teacher education, note that while most teachers working in schools worldwide have received some preparation, not all have received adequate preparation. In fact, many have received none at all. In India in 1996, for example, there were about 240,000 teachers who were not fully qualified. There also are severe teacher shortages in many countries, the problem being especially severe in South Asia and Africa. Even in developed countries where there are sufficient numbers of teachers, as in the U.S.A., many are unqualified or underqualified to teach specialized subjects like mathematics and science. ICT is being used in a wide variety of ways to support both preservice and inservice teacher education. In Africa, UNESCO is developing a large distance education to help eight countries train teachers and principals unreached by traditional training.

Also in Africa, education ministers from six Southern African Commonwealth countries have signed an accord to co-develop distance education programs with a priority given to the in-service training or teachers in science, mathematics, and technology. In Australia, the Faculty of Education at the University of Wollongong is linking teachers and postgraduate students directly to lecturers through email networks and provides online support to teachers in schools. TeacherNet UK, an independent organization, offers teachers the opportunity to develop an online profile of their interests, needs, and prior achievements, and then matches the individual participants accredited professional development programs. TeacherNet UK also enables peer support and mentoring through email and web-based discussion groups. In Iceland, the University College of Education offers a Bachelor of Education (BEd) degree via the Icelandic Education Network. In Denmark, teacher education is being conducted using ICT including computer-mediated conferencing (CMC) supplemented by satellite-based teleconferencing, multimedia and standard computer-based training. And, in a final example of how ICT is being used to support teacher education, the TRENDS, a collaborative effort of the seven European Union countries, is developing an in-service, school-based teachers training system based on multimedia and network technologies.

Teacher training

How computers are used in education depends on the pedagogical competence and technical skills of the teaching staff who must know how to exploit these modern technologies in pedagogically meaningful ways. Regional, national, and local plans for ICT in education typically include provisions for teacher training. ICT training for teachers has at least two aspects—technical training and preparation to integrate ICT use into the curricula. First, teachers need technical training to learn how to use and maintain ICT equipment and software. Such technical training is being offered to teachers in a wide variety of ways. Preservice university-based courses, inservice workshops, commercial training programs, and other opportunities abound, many of which make use of ICT to deliver instruction. Second, as "integration of technologies into curricula requires changes of huge magnitude", training in how to integrate ICT-use into the curriculum is necessary. Such instruction should including effective teaching methods with ICT and the use of discipline specific applications:

Most faculty members say they don't have the time or skills to experiment with the World Wide Web, let alone try complicated courseware, streaming video, or on-line message boards. They need sophisticated guidance, which most computer-help desks and student assistants can't provide. And they need more than a computing center's basic training in how to use Windows or word-processing software. Many promising approaches are being developed to provide such support for faculty. In an expensive but effective approach, several universities have established "expert partners" programs. People who fill the jobs have one thing in common: a hybrid expertise that blends academic computing with college teaching". Staff who are both qualified academics within a discipline, and who have expertise using ICT for instruction, are hired "to provide faculty on-site, intradepartmental consulting and support in information and instructional technology for academic purposes to foster their awareness and use of technological resources, both within and without the University".

Training methodologies vary, but "training of trainers" models are common and, in most instances, may be more cost-effective than on-site, small group or individual ICT training. In such programs, "teacher-leaders" are selected by a variety of criteria, usually including prior experience with ICT in education, staff development expertise, and commitment to the program by school and district administration. These individuals receive intensive training courses to master technical details and approaches to integrating ICT into the curricula. Once trained, they return to their educational institutions and provide ICT training and support for their peers. Such programs may also include on-going, long-term support for the trainers including site visits, computer-based conferences, and email mentoring. In large geographical areas, the responsibility for such training and on-going support may be delegated to regional ICT consortia, coordinated by a central administrative body. For example, the U.S. Department of Education has funded six Regional Technology in Education Consortia "to help states, local educational agencies, teachers, school library and media personnel, administrators, and other education entities successfully integrate technologies into kindergarten through 12th grade (K-12) classrooms, library media centers, and other educational settings, including adult literacy centers".

In an innovative and less inexpensive approach, students are being enlisted to provide ICT support and training for teachers. At Wake Forest University in the United States, incoming freshmen are hired and trained to work as Student Technology AdvisoRS (STARS). STARS are assigned faculty members to help implement ICT-based matters. Also in the U.S., a consortium of educational associations has launched a national grassroots to train public school teachers to use computers and the Internet. The 21st Century Teachers hopes to recruit 100,000 educators this year to train their peers.

In the United Kingdom, the ICT Training Initiative of the Teacher Training Agency (TTA) offers a combination of technical and discipline-specific applications training. The TTA, working with other educational organizations and a commercial company, will produce a package—including CD-ROM, video and paper-based materials—to help teachers identify their specific training and development needs in the use of ICT in teaching their subjects. Starting in April 1999, training - some of it Internet-based - will be offered to enable existing teachers to acquire the ICT knowledge, understanding, and skills which will be expected of all newly qualified teachers entering the profession from 1999. In Australia, the Connecting Teachers to the Future, is providing teachers with training and a laptop computer, modem, and an Internet account "to empower teachers with personal skills in the use of information and communications technologies and to help them enhance the curriculum they develop for their students". Technical Support Although standard service agreements, purchased separately or included in the purchase of ICT equipment and software, typically cover regular maintenance and repair costs, and may even include email or telephone support, such arrangements may fall short of what is necessary in educational settings. Without adequate technical support, schools have experienced "large workloads for existing staff, maintenance backlogs, and reduced computer use because computers were out of service". The provision of on-site, timely technical support may be critical to the success of an ICT-based educational program:

> There appears to be general agreement among observers that, at least in the foreseeable future, schools that are attempting to implement technology on a wide scale need to have on-site technical assistance. Although some sites have attempted to make do with help from a knowledgeable teacher volunteer or with part-time services from a district technology coordinator, such arrangements are often unsatisfactory. Like all of us, teachers trying to use technology in their classrooms want technical help on demand. Controlling a classroom full of students in the midst of some activity that requires technology when the system goes down requires flexibility and skill. If technical problems arise frequently and teachers have to wait hours, days, or weeks to get them resolved, they will abandon their efforts to incorporate technology.

In universities, such support may take the form of technical staff assigned to a computer center, "media center," or "distance learning center." In schools, knowledgeable peers, students, volunteers, specialized computer lab teachers are providing such support, and, less frequently, trained technical staff located either within the school or district office. In an example of students' expertise being utilized, members of the American Technology Honor Society (ATHS) provide ICT support and training for faculty members at their schools. In an example of how volunteers may provide such support, tech corp, a U.S. based, non-profit organization, draws volunteers from the local communities who conduct teacher training seminars, serve as technology mentors to students and teachers, repair and install computers, participate in technology planning, and assist with the integration of technology into the curriculum.

ICT implementation in education is a difficult, expensive, and complex undertaking that must consider a host of issues including infrastructure, curricula changes, teacher training, technical support, and so on. Such an undertaking, especially on a national level, requires careful planning. Numerous developed and developing countries have implemented national strategies and plans for education that include ICT.

Osin, summarizing the experiences ofmeant to introduce computers into the educational systems of developing countries, offers prudent advice. He warns against beginning purchasing computers, which often results in "a waste of money that could be put to better use". Instead, he advocates an eight step planning process beginning with gathering together the necessary expertise in an Advisory Committee that will define and implement a plan beginning with the careful execution of pilot. Osin also recommends training a cadre of instructors for teacher training, introducing computers into teachers colleges, and conducting both formative and summative evaluations of the pilot before attempting a large-scale ICT implementation. Beyond planning, national governments have a role to play helping remove political and economic roadblocks that prevent sharing educational resources between countries. Distance education, advocate: "Courses offered globally should encourage broad international participation and have sliding scale tuition policies. Sharing in developing educational materials and courses saves the duplication of time and effort and conserves valuable national resources".

Employers and universities are now drawing both staff members and students from all corners of the globe. Consequently, they face new challenges in evaluating course work done at, and degrees earned from, unknown institutions in other countries. While accreditation has typically been controlled by individual countries, the globalization of distance education has created a whole new challenge in accreditation and certification of learning. The Global Alliance for Transnational Education (GATE), an international alliance of higher education, government, and business, as one effort to carry out the formidable task of creating a global certification and review process for education delivered across borders. Government intervention may also help assure affordable ICT access for education. For example, telecommunications rates may be regulated to assure economical ICT access to educational institutions. In late 1996, the U.S. Congress enacted the Telecommunications Act of 1996.

The universal service section of the law, Section 254, will help US schools and libraries obtain access to telecommunications services and technologies at discounted rates. And tax incentives, such as the 21st Century Classrooms Act for Private Technology Investment, enacted by the U.S. Congress in 1997, are a potent means to encourage corporate ICT equipment donations to educational institutions. The Act allows companies to deduct the full price of a computer donated to a school within two years of purchase. However, because ICTs are rapidly evolving, national educational policies on ICT, once put in place, "have to be regularly updated if they are to respond adequately to the challenge of effectively exploiting these constant changes to the technologies and their applications".

Intellectual property refers to original or novel creations of the human mind. Intellectual property rights give the creator exclusive right to use such creations for a specified period of time. These creations may include literary works, industrial designs, musical compositions and arrangements, paintings, trade secrets, sculptures, computer programs, performances, inventions, and so forth. Copyright, trademarks, and patents are legal methods to protect such rights. The creation, maintenance, protection and transfer of intellectual property assets are increasingly important in today's global economy. The availability of ICT and the ease with which the fruits of human creativity may be duplicated, incorporated into multimedia products, and transmitted worldwide has led to increasing efforts to govern such use. In an era when every student and teacher is a potential publisher of multimedia materials that incorporate the works of others, information and training about the ethical use of intellectual property should be an important component of efforts to bring ICT use into the classroom. Without international laws protecting intellectual property, and mechanisms by which to "meter" charges for its use, efforts to share resources globally will be inhibited.

The web-based system enables researchers to request articles from more than 10,000 Chinese academic journals housed in libraries throughout China, Hong Kong, and Taiwan while scholars from those countries have direct access to articles from most American journals. However, once requested electronically, the articles must still be printed and mailed because of publishers fears that copies will be distributed illegally over the Internet. In universities, copyright concerns may be inhibiting the creation and use of ICT-based instructional materials. For example, increasing use of ICT has led to a re-examination of the question of ownership of materials produced by faculty:

> The ownership of intellectual property is among the most widely debated issues on university campuses today, and those debates go far beyond the distance learning issue itself. Typically, in settings other than universities, it is well settled that the material created by employees within the scope of their employment is owned by the employer. However, the unique mission of the university, academic tradition, and the essential principles of academic freedom have led faculty to claim that they own the material they create. Historically, many university administrations have asserted institutional ownership, but then allowed, or not challenged, the faculty position with regard to copyrights, at least in part because both the financial "cost" and the value of most copyrightable creations were usually insignificant when compared with the cost and value of patentable inventions. But as the potential value of copyrighted material escalates, particularly with the advent of multimedia software, and as financial resources diminish, many universities are revisiting who owns the intellectual property created by faculty.

International efforts are underway to develop global standards and agreements that will protect intellectual property rights while developing methods to allow access to, and sharing of, intellectual property. For example, The United Nations' World Intellectual Property Organization (WIPO), an intergovernmental organization with 171 participating countries.

ICT itself is being used to provide assistance and information to educators and others interested in intellectual property laws. WIPO has just begun work on a global information network using the Internet that will facilitate the storage and rapid exchange of intellectual property information between all interested parties in governments and the private sector in member States. A global association of 152 independent law firms, offers a website directory with links to hundreds of legal guides about countries around the world, most of which contain information concerning intellectual property laws. Other organizations, such as the U.S. Franklin Pierce Law Center, Ruslaw in Russia, and the Australian Copyright Council, offer websites with information about national laws governing intellectual property rights.

Equity of access, put simply, means that all people, whether rich or poor, living in a developed or developing country, male or female, have access to the benefits of ICT-use. While this ideal is widely supported, it is a long way from realized.

Access to and use of ICT is still predominately a phenomenon in developed, wealthier countries. This disparity leads to concerns that ICT will broaden and deepen the economic, educational, social, and political gaps that divide the developing from the developed nations.

Poor countries - and poor people - differ from rich ones not only because they have less capital, but because they have less knowledge. This inequity has been recognized by international agencies such as the United Nations and World Bank, and governments of the developed countries. As was noted earlier, UNESCO, through the Learning Without Frontiers (LWF) and other programs, is helping organize and finance pilot ICT in education in developing countries. National governments in developed countries, too, are taking measures to assist in the creation of ICT infrastructure in developing countries. For example, the Clinton administration in the United States is pushing for funding to help developing countries link to the Internet for commercial and educational purposes. But huge inequities exist that will be difficult to overcome. If inequities in access to ICTs in developing countries can be overcome, it may enable their citizens to leapfrog over economic and educational barriers developing countries need not reinvent the wheel - or the computer, or treatment for malaria. Rather than re-create existing knowledge, poor countries have the option of acquiring and adapting much knowledge already available in the richer countries.

With communications costs plummeting, transferring knowledge is cheaper than ever. ... Expanding telecommunications holds the promise to improve every developing country's capacity to absorb knowledge, for example by providing opportunities high-quality, low-cost adult learning. Expanding telecommunications capability also provides an avenue to reach distant markets with locally produced products while at the same time educating others about local cultures. The Catdang Village Project in Vietnam is using ICT to reach a worldwide audience with information about local cultures while exploiting economic opportunities. The web-based, selling locally produced lacquered bamboo baskets, is aimed at "providing sustainable regenerative income for village artisans and their families". While economically oriented, the website contains cultural information and images of Catdang; a small village located over a hundred miles south of Hanoi. Other inequities in ICT access exist. The poor are less likely to have access to ICT, in or out of school. Even in the developed world, access to the benefits of these technologies has by no means been equally available throughout all sectors of the population, with certain sections of society remaining deprived of many of the advantages offered by ICTs".

Schools in high-income areas were much more likely to have lower pupil-computer ratios and Internet access. Throughout the developing world, the situation is much worse. Access to even basic communications technologies is limited to a few. In South Asia and Sub-Saharan Africa, there are about 1.5 telephone lines per 100 people compared to 64 per hundred in the United States. In conclusion, when considering ICT, "threat and opportunity are opposite sides of the same coin". ICT has the potential to greatly enhance the information-base, knowledge, and educational opportunities of the poor and of developing countries. However, such benefits will depend upon whether there is equitable access to ICT. If not, ICT may increase the gap between the haves and have-nots of the world.

Gender According to UNICEF, over 130 million children of school age in the developing world are growing up without access to basic education, of whom nearly two of every three are female. If lucky or privileged enough to attend school, a number of studies have shown females are far less likely to enroll in science, mathematics, computer science and engineering courses.

In the winter 1997-98 surveys, 44% of the Web users were women, up from 21% in September 1995. As a portion of the overall US population, 3% of adult women in the September1995 survey said they logged onto the Web compared to 12% of men. Research now shows that

26% of all American women use the Web, as do 35% of men. However, U.S. women, too, choose ICT-related careers less frequently, and are more likely to change career fields: "Women are leaving or avoiding computer careers in droves, citing discrimination by male co-workers, few role models, family-unfriendly work environments and a general sense that the field is irrelevant to their interests ... The most immediate effect is to worsen the nation's shortage of high-tech workers"

ICT is also being used both to provide information about gender issues to teachers, and to encourage women's use of information and communications technologies. For example, the Women'sNet in South Africa offers a variety of information on women's issues and is planning to offer an Internet training program for women in the near future. The Ada Project (TAP) and its TAP Junior offshoot at Yale University in the United States, serves as a clearinghouse for information and resources relating to women in computing. The Center for Women and Information Technology at the University of Maryland Baltimore County (UMBC) is dedicated to addressing the technology gender gap. Its website includes curricular resources, news articles on gender and technology, and links to sites focusing on women, girls, and information technology.

Whether the changing language demographics on the Internet will result in English becoming a common language for ICT-enabled discourse, or will result in a "tower of ICT-enabled babble" is an open question. Language translation software may offer some solutions to this problem, but such technologies are far from mature. We should not lose sight of the potential of these applications for enhancing global understanding. ... Dance, music, collected memories, and shared imaginings can provide a common global language." Paradoxically, despite fears of cultural imperialism on the Internet, use of ICT is also seen as a means to protect and project cultural, religious, and other differences: There is an important counter-effect or internal contradiction in our global, Net-based information society: simultaneously with the rise of global networked society there is an increase in national, ethnic, and religious identity politics and the resistances to globalization inherent in these movements. Many of the identity groups represent themselves as explicit points of resistance to a global system of any kind while simultaneously using the tools of globalization.

ICT is also enhancing the ability of people from different cultures to interact with and create cultural materials. Whether the Internet will create a "Global Village" in which all participants' cultures and languages are equally valued, or foster an "invasion" by which diverse cultures and languages will be electronically subjugated, is an open question.

Although connectivity, including access to remote resources, is a major beneficial feature distinguishing newer ICTs from old, such access has negative aspects. Whether - and to what extent - the free exchange of information will take place using ICT is being widely debated, with the transborder nature of ICT adding new, complex dimensions to such discussions. Concerns about pornography, violence, and crime on the Internet are widespread, and Internet political activism is also raising alarm in some countries. Anti-censorship and pro-censorship organizations are carrying the debate to a worldwide audience through ICT.

ICT manufacturers are introducing ways of overcoming the problem of school children being able to access content deemed inappropriate by local schools and parents. Such tools include "proxy servers" and "filtering" software. A proxy server is a computer on the school network on which educators can store pre-screened and approved information. Use of a proxy server limits student access to only those resources placed on the local server. "Filtering" software scans incoming information for specific words, phrases, or websites and blocks access to banned content.

Beyond the questions raised by pornographic, violent, politically unsuitable, or criminal information on the Internet, another issue facing educators is the validity of the information available on the Internet. "While a wide realm of information is available on the Internet, it must be remembered that there is no monitoring agency and no restriction on posting false information for all to see". Students searching the Internet for information about the question of life in outer space are just as likely to find arguments based on religious believes, paranormal cults, as on scientific evidence. It appears unlikely that this situation can be resolved. As Peace recommends, "Care must be taken by the instructor that students are made well aware of this situation, and that policies are developed to deal with the inevitable dilemma raised by a student citing incorrect information, found legitimately on the Internet, in support of a flawed argument".

As we trust has been demonstrated in this chapter, the use of newer, digital ICTs - because of the ability to integrate multiple media, interactivity, flexibility of use, and connectivity -are inspiring remarkable transformations in education around the world. These transformations hold promise for the improvement of the lives of the rich and of the poor, whether living in developed and developing countries. We have chosen to focus on existing, widespread uses of ICTs in education, but advances in wireless telecommunications, virtual reality, pervasive computing, artificial intelligence, speech recognition, and "next generation" networking technologies promise to remodel today's educational applications as comprehensively as the computer revolutionized yesterday's. If we can claim to have detected any "theme" in our overview of ICT in education worldwide, it is this - ICT is neutral, human choices will determine how ICT will be used and whether the revolution in information and communications technologies will benefit all humanity.

This is true at the micro-level, in the choices teachers make when deciding whether and how to use ICT in the classroom, to the macro-level, by the choices international, regional, and national governmental and non-governmental organizations (NGOs) make to support, or not, ICT access in formal and informal educational settings. Of course, we hope the information contained within this chapter (which will no doubt be out-of-date shortly after publication) can help individual decision-makers reach informed choices about ICT in education. But more than that, we hope the remarkable developments in this chapter have touched the imagination and helped inspire a sense of urgency to act to so that all children may benefit.

5

Governing ICTs

In most countries, the electronic media and telecommunications were directly owned by governments or subject to interventionist government regulatory regimes well into the 1980s. As a result, national cultural and economic policies shaped the development of the world's communications for over a century. Some theorists of the digital revolution suggest that nation states will lose their relevance in a borderless future cyberspace, where transactions and communications will occur beyond the reach of government regulation or control.

There are two common versions of this particular view of the future. Some see the decline of national regulation as a positive step towards the exercise of greater individual freedom in communications and more direct democratic participation. A variant of this view is that a digital enfeeblement of government will only strengthen the powerful transnational commercial interests that are already dominant. The latter view serves as a reminder that it is national governments which constitutionally represent the individual citizen. An alternative approach is to see the new technologies as 'embedded in the real world', as the Internet was once described by one of its pioneers.

Without ignoring the potential of new communications systems, this approach emphasizes both the economic, legal and policy factors that influence the emergence and adoption of these services. Innovation in communications occurs within a longer historical pattern of evolution. Recognizing the fact that few, if any, governments will have the capacity or inclination to control every aspect of increasingly sophisticated communications systems does not mean the end of long-standing responsibilities. Governments will need to balance the potential benefits of new information and communication technologies with the threats that they pose. Questions of preserving privacy, protecting children, and enforcing the rights of authors are more complex in the new media, but they have not disappeared.

The transition to digital broadcasting transmission systems in developed societies, and the proliferation of subscription television, is likely to lead to much greater diversity in media services, including interactive data transmission, high definition television, more targeted special interest programming, pay-per-view programming and electronic commerce facilities. The technical key here is the expansion of bandwidth, the capacity of a communications channel to convey information. The shortage of frequencies is much less a factor in limiting services than in the past. This factor has important ramifications for policy: in the context of a generally more liberal, market-oriented approach to media and telecommunications, spectrum scarcity can no longer function as a primary rationale for close government regulation of electronic media. At the same time, the diversification of electronic media appears to challenge the traditional unifying, 'nation-building' missions of public sector broadcasting services.

Global computer networks have only recently become mass communication systems in their own right, with the worldwide spread of small, cheap and easy-to-use desktop computers, which are now in use in almost all areas of human activity. New telecommunications technology made it possible to adapt the telephone system for data transmission. New kinds of software expanded enormously both the variety and the purpose of networked information: beyond their traditional messaging and database functions, computer networks became systems for publishing and distributing information of all kinds.

As their sophistication increased, networks ceased to be strictly text-based. High-resolution colour images, video, and sound documents have become commonplace network resources. Applications in the form of browser plug-ins, Java 'applets' and proprietary components are also becoming commonplace.

At the same time, the world's computer networks have become more interconnected, and therefore more readily accessible. The network of networks that has evolved into the Internet uses a decentralized, packet-switched architecture to link computers in over two hundred countries. Proprietary online services - the self-contained, subscription-based, market-oriented systems of the early 1990s - were by the mid-1990s forced to connect to the Internet since many were failing to compete with the larger, freer, public system.

But while these technologies have developed quickly, and the ultimate objective of an accessible, low-cost global information infrastructure has become available, the consequences of their diffusion will take much longer to recognize and respond to. Actual applications and benefits remain hazy. It is not yet clear that greater diversity in services will deliver greater diversity in content. Critical issues which are yet to be resolved include the scope of the public domain in the digital environment, and the ability of governments to adapt existing systems of regulation.

Policy Responses

Since the beginning of this decade at least, governments and international organizations around the world have devoted substantial resources to understanding the implications of 'the digital revolution' in communications. Indeed such is the volume of this material, and the enthusiasm with which it embraces technologically-driven change, that we can scarcely doubt that the very concept of an 'information revolution' must be in part the product of official policy discourse, despite the advocates of a cyberspace without rulers.

The phenomenon of governments embracing new communications technologies has several facets. In highly industrialized societies, the early and middle years of the 1990s were characterized by a 'visionary' fascination with the promise of future interactive broadband delivery systems. National government documents such as Denmark's Info-Society 2000, the United States' National Information Infrastructure and Global Information Infrastructure reports, and Singapore's IT2000 fell into this category; at the international level, the European Union's Bangemann Report and the G-7 summit's Information Society conference were comparable.

These visionary information policies 'tend[ed] to be more statements of aspiration than realistic policies aimed at achievable goals'. Yet these grand if somewhat unfocused visions still shape information policies around the world. New technologies were seen as the key to improved delivery of essential government services, especially in health and education. They were also seen as major driving forces for economic growth, offering improved productivity and new demand for skilled labour.

In general terms, governments accepted without critical scrutiny the potential benefits of information technology, focusing on the perceived need for a broadband infrastructure. At the same time, the absence of this infrastructure was uniformly seen as a significant disadvantage from which other problems flowed: deficiencies in technological skills, uncompetitive industries, low growth rates. The analysis was circular.

A broadband infrastructure was not, in fact, necessary for many practical improvements in communications, either in the West or elsewhere. The success of the narrowband Internet, for example, rests on its accessibility through standard twisted-pair telephone lines and comparatively inexpensive modems. The rise of the Internet has made possible the proliferation of network computing earlier than the most ambitious prophets of the information revolution imagined; but it has done so without the expensive broadband infrastructure which was so widely considered a prerequisite for information societies. Nevertheless, the best of these broad policy statements have had a number of important effects.

First, they gave information policies greater political priority. What was once an obscure dimension of Teledemocracy is the adaptation of Internet-based information tools by government, business, and civil society to create an advanced participatory form of democracy. In its purely theoretical form, teledemocracy is the use of the Internet to produce an informed and publicly active citizenship. But in its current form, teledemocracy is a misused and misconstrued term: while the prefix tele explicitly means 'distance' or 'way of', adding the conception of the Internet gives teledemocracy a more technical characteristic.

Empowerment is the foundation of teledemocracy. In order to fulfill the ultimate goal of empowering citizens, two measures must be put in place:

— All citizens must have access to information tools. This highlights the importance of universal access to knowledge and participation in the Information Society.

— Government, business, and civil society must have a strong and committed Web presence. Teledemocracy cannot advance properly without the necessary balance between these three groups.

In existing democracies, the process starts locally with a virtual administrative body which consists of Web sites sponsored by local governments to facilitate exchange between elected officials and local citizens. Experiments of this kind are being carried out all over the United States, in parts of Europe, and other democratic countries. The Web sites are a dedicated forum for public policy debate, government outreach program, and in some cases, replace conventional mail with e-mail. Teledemocracy is further promoted through cyber-neighbourhoods, which are connected communities with access for each individual family, and cyberparties, which are representative groups that encourage online public participation. Both serve the function of increasing citizen partnership, through direct, active lobbying by citizens.

Online lobbying is no longer restricted to government and business; informed and empowered individuals may take an active role in voicing their opinions. In non-democratic countries and governments in transition, teledemocracy is practiced differently: through teledemocratization, which is the use of Internet-based information tools to promote knowledge-sharing among citizens and to organize citizen opposition groups. In turn, it may be used to circumvent oppressive regulatory efforts and facilitate discussion among civil societies, government and business.

The effect of teledemocratization cannot be underestimated: the technical aspects of the network allow for technical solutions to offset government propaganda, censorship, and other repressive measures. Such is the case with Radio B92 in Belgrade. When shut down for its anti-government broadcasts, the station moved onto the Internet, and was rebroadcast into Yugoslavia by Radio Free Europe and Voice of America. It has become the sole source of independent reporting in Yugoslavia and a rallying point for democratic opposition.

Teledemocracy is only beginning to gain recognition for what it is: a valuable tool to produce an empowered and active society. While the theoretical evolution is still in its infancy, functional teledemocracy is already spreading to many parts of the world. Virtual local administrations are being envisaged and constructed, citizens are becoming more active in communities through cyber-neighbourhoods, and government regulations are circumvented by the technical solutions offered by the Internet. In step with the advancement of information and communication technologies, teledemocracy may well be a fast-developing, governing characteristic of the Information Society.

Governments have begun to make strategic connections between issues that were hitherto fragmented across traditional administrative boundaries - issues such as data protection, intellectual property, electronic commerce, and computers in school education.

Some of these early government responses did adopt a wider social perspective on the possibilities and consequences of the new communications environment. Denmark's Info-Society 2000 policy, for example, looked beyond the provision of infrastructure. It was concerned with how a future 'info-society' might retain the distinctive Danish characteristics of equity, democratic participation, and openness. It was much more concerned with applications than the supply of technology, and addressed the ways in which the public sector could cooperate with business. It emphasized the need to consider questions of access to government information. These issues were developed alongside an agenda for micro-economic reform, which concentrated on the need to liberalize Danish telecommunications.

The wide-ranging information policies developed in the mid-1990s have led to more concrete, if somewhat scaled-down, programmes for change. The aspirational thinking of the mid-1990s may have diverted attention from such practical policy questions as access to the Internet, improvements in basic telecommunications, and the development of real services and industries. But these issues have recently become the focus of policy attention, especially since the emergence of the Internet as the most important and fastest-growing global computer network. Singapore's IT2000 plan provides an example.

Like so many other visions of the information age, IT2000 was aimed squarely at a universally accessible broadband network. The rise of the Internet changed this priority, forcing Singapore's National Computer Board to concentrate on the emergence of markets for interactive services rather than the development of the enabling technologies. This in turn meant an analysis of Singapore's particular strengths in fields such as logistics, transport and government information provision. The increasing pervasiveness of information and communication technologies in the everyday activities of citizens has spurred governments to develop policies aimed at ensuring maximum community participation.

In *A Strategic Framework for the Information Economy*, the Australian government states its commitment to provide all Australians with open and equitable access to information available online as a way of securing 'a strong democratic, informed and inclusive society', and to avoid 'a social polarization between the so-called "information rich" and "information poor"'.

The challenge highlighted by the Secretary-General of the United Nations is to use the technologies to make information available to all and harness its democratizing power. However, as discussed later on, citizens in many countries do not have the opportunity to share in the benefits of the new technologies. Participation of developing countries, in particular, is being impeded by a lack of adequate communication infrastructure and relatively high computing costs. These issues were highlighted at a seminar sponsored by the United Nations Population Fund and the Government of Turkey in December 1998. The seminar also discussed the need for policies to address social and gender inequality to prevent information and communication technologies from further marginalizing disadvantaged groups. Even so, available information and communication technologies are being used in developing countries as tools in advocacy and to promote social change. For example, in the area of reproductive health services, new media are being used to build political commitment and community support. In Senegal, youth leaders have organized cyber-cafes where young people can discuss life-planning skills and connect with the world's youth. Ecuador has a service using the Internet to provide news to community radio stations. There is a website linking a network of Turkish NGOs against gender-based violence. In South America, distance learning programmes are offered on population and reproductive health.

Framework for Governance

ICTs provide comparatively decentralized and open environments which appear to promote these rights. Networked environments like the Internet allow individuals to create their own content and interact with a large audience worldwide at relatively low cost. This in turn increases the diversity of information and views that are expressed by and accessible to users around the world.

The new technologies can assist the democratic process by facilitating greater accountability and transparency of governments: official documents are increasingly being made available on line and opportunities for direct communication with elected representatives are being created. A concomitant of this situation is that the medium may be used to generate and disseminate content, which may itself be seen to be anti-democratic and offensive to many that receive it.

The characteristics of the new media mean that, unlike traditional broadcast media, there are higher expectations of individual freedom and autonomy. However, as more parts of the networked world and the real world overlap, the need for governance increases. Numerous commentators have highlighted the difficulties of governance in a computer-generated public domain that has no territorial boundaries or physical attributes and is in perpetual use.

Democratic governance requires public interests and values to be reflected within the rule-making processes. In attempting to meet these challenges and retain the democratic characteristics of networked environments, there has been a tendency toward a governance model that is decentralized or self-regulatory in nature, especially in Australia, Canada, Japan, the United Kingdom, the United States and many European countries, particularly under the influence of the European Commission.

A number of international organizations are also influencing the emerging framework for governance of new information and communications mediums, including the United Nations (UN), the Organization for Economic Cooperation and Development (OECD), the

World Trade Organization, the International Standards Organization, and the World Intellectual Property Organization.

The OECD is actively contributing to a global framework for electronic commerce. A Ministerial Conference on electronic commerce held in October 1998 in Ottawa proposed an action plan to bring notions of physical world governance into the networked world. The action plan is organized along the following lines:

— building trust for users and consumers, so that the safeguards which provide confidence in the physical marketplace are adjusted to instill equivalent confidence in the digital marketplace;

— establishing ground rules for the digital marketplace, including providing protection that is as effective as that provided by legal and commercial frameworks in the physical world;

— enhancing the information infrastructure for electronic commerce, including creating effective competition in telecommunications markets;

— maximizing the benefits of electronic commerce.

The emergence of an information society, with new systems and modes of expression, representation and action, is a major challenge for UNESCO and its Member States. As part of its response to this phenomenon, the Organization is striving to 'help its Member States frame integrated policies and strategies, taking account of the convergence of telecommunications, information technology and the electronic media, which will enable them to adapt themselves to this new technological environment and take advantage of the opportunities it offers'.

The most striking aspect of this new environment is cyberspace, which is also known as 'information highways'. This new electronic space, open to all forms of expression, information exchange and transactions, is becoming progressively accessible to an increasing number of people, whatever their age, geocultural origins or occupation. The ICTs which form the infrastructure of cyberspace, more particularly the Internet, are used for many different purposes, for the best and the worst. This new environment transcends state borders and largely escapes national juridictions.

UNESCO's governing bodies, the General conference and the Executive board, have urged the Organization to take a leading role to ensure that education, science and culture are given adequate intellectual space on the information highways. UNESCO's strategy is being developed around two complementary main lines of action. The first is to encourage international interdisciplinary reflection on the ethical, cultural, legal and social issues which characterize the emerging information society and, second, to promote the use of information technologies for the development of education, science, culture and communication.

In collaboration with producers and users of the ICTs and providers of cyberspace information and services, the Organization promotes the ethical values and legal principles essential for a democratic and participatory information society. In particular, UNESCO's efforts are directed towards promoting universal access to information and creating the conditions under which the information society can guarantee respect for privacy and personal data, enrich all lives, include the excluded and disadvantaged, ensure cultural pluralism and be free from violence, pornography, paedophilia, racism, alienating ideologies and criminality. These are the objectives of the Project on ethical and sociocultural challenges of the new information society.

The Organization is also working to ensure that ICTs are used more effectively to foster freedom of expression, the free flow of information, access to knowledge for all throughout life, scientific research, artistic creativity, the protection and enhancement of the heritage and the common good. The programmes being implemented contribute to these ends in different ways and include: the diversification of educational services, especially through distance education; the establishment of networks and discussion forums on the Internet for educational, scientific and cultural communities; the digitization and online presentation of the cultural heritage, the organization of virtual curricula, libraries and laboratories; 'online governance'; the provision of computer hardware and software and means of access to networks; and the training of electronic network managers and trainers in informatics, telematics and multimedia.

Together with its international, regional and national partners, UNESCO has taken several initiatives in organizing a series of conferences and expert meetings worldwide. These include the African Regional Symposium on Telematics for Development, the Conference on Electronic Publishing in Science, organized with the International Council for Science, the International UNESCO Symposium on Copyright and Communication in the Information Society, the second International Congress on Education and Informatics, the regional symposium on The Arab World and the Information Society, the Asia-Pacific regional meeting of experts on A Legal Framework for Cyberspace, the Expert Meeting on Cyberspace Law and the two infoethics congresses held in Monaco in 1997 and 1998. To fulfil its role as a platform for international debate, UNESCO has initiated an Observatory on the Information Society on the World Wide Web with a focus on ethical, legal, social and cultural aspects.

Education and IT

Technology has a major impact in the field of education. It demonstrates more clearly than any other the influence of information policy, and the efforts of governments to address the problems identified by information policy. The recent OECD Information Technology Outlook made an explicit link between increased government emphasis on information technologies and the transition of OECD economies to 'knowledge-based' economies. According to the report, it was imperative for nations that their people have the knowledge and skills needed for participation in a knowledge-based society.

In the United States, which is often to assumed to be far advanced in the introduction of information technology into the classroom, a recent Federal Report noted that 'few schools have adequate numbers of modern computers or access to the Internet, and relatively few teachers are prepared to use technology effectively. Further, access to computers and other technologies is not enough; integration of technology into the curriculum is also needed'.

A recent Irish government report describes what it calls the 'down side' of new technologies. A host of potentially illegal uses of the Internet have emerged as major issues for national policy and international coordination. These include:

— *Piracy of intellectual property*: the infringement of copyright in cultural property; the infringement of moral rights of authors; and the illegal distribution of copyright works such as books or videotapes.

— *Gambling*: the emergence of unlicensed and unregulated Internet casinos.

— *Invasion of privacy*: unsolicited electronic communications; misuse of personal information in databases; theft of personal information; unauthorized interception of personal communications.

— *Commercial crimes*: fraud, including credit card piracy.

— *Harmful communications*: illegal material, including child pornography, violent material, and racial or religious vilification; defamatory publications.

— *Hacking or cracking*: illegal entry into private or government computers; theft of data or malicious damage to data.

One of the great attractions of the Internet remains its capacity for comparatively free global communication, including communication to and from countries where open discourse may be suppressed. It can collapse geographical space, apparently transcending boundaries.

Information services in the field of illegal or harmful material

Another most significant area of need for regulating new information services is in the field of illegal or harmful material. A recent UNESCO Expert Meeting on Paedophilia on the Internet is one example in this area. We know that whether information is considered harmful or not depends on the cultural, religious and social context in which it is circulated. Within and between nations, these standards vary enormously.

At local, regional and national levels, governments have long sought to control the distribution of material deemed harmful. Clearly the task has become much more complicated in the age of global digital networks. It is no longer possible for government censors to mandate the classification of all the material that may be available in any jurisdiction.

It is no longer possible to physically police the information that crosses jurisdictional borders; and while screening technologies may be effective in some circumstances, data has the capacity to slip across a frontier in many forms and from many sources including international phone lines, Internet services, satellite transmissions and broadcasting.

Many countries have constructed classification or censorship systems which work by making distinctions between different kinds of analogue media, based on assumptions about the different patterns of circulation of, for example, books and broadcast, free to air television. How are these graduated systems of classification or censorship to be applied to digital media? The question which arises is whether it is too simplistic to merely insist that 'what is illegal off line is illegal on line'. There are dilemmas in balancing the principle of freedom of expression against citizens' rights to be protected from illegal or harmful material.

A recent Human Rights Watch report demonstrates the range of methods employed to control content on the Internet. Some countries, such as Ireland and Australia, are moving towards the adoption of co-regulatory structures, sharing responsibility between national agencies and industry for raising public awareness, responding appropriately to illegal material when necessary, and providing effective complaints procedures.

Co-regulation is being facilitated by technologies that make the development of tools such as content labelling and complaint hotlines possible. Other national authorities, such as those in Saudi Arabia, Bahrain and Malaysia, seek to control the Internet more tightly, often by restricting access to the global network through a limited number of gateways which may then be monitored and configured to block access to sites considered harmful or undesirable.

The report notes the widespread international endorsement of technical tools to assist in the regulation of content on the World Wide Web. In particular, the labelling technology known as Platform for Internet Content Selection (PICS), first developed by the World Wide Web Consortium, has attracted great interest in Europe, Australia, Asia and North America.

PICS provides a means for the labelling, and subsequent filtering, of Web content which may be both more standardized and more powerful than simple site-blocking software. One of its features is that such labels may be generated, published and used by anyone: it brings an effective classificatory apparatus within the reach of schools, libraries, community groups, parents, or any interested party.

The PICS protocol can support a variety of ratings and labelling systems so they can be tailored to the needs of each user, and allows content rating to reflect the vast range of cultural perspectives on appropriate access to certain material. In this way it belongs to that tendency of thought about the Internet which stands in opposition to the notion of a distinct and remote digital space, separated from the daily circumstances and places of its use.

Instead PICS works from the assumption that 'the Internet is embedded in the real world'. Supporters of PICS have pointed to its feature of enabling, and in fact encouraging, a multiplicity of classification standards as the means to retain local control and responsibility over content. PICS is therefore seen, in the European Union and elsewhere, as a means of preserving cultural and social diversity within a global system.

Organizations in several countries have established labelling schemes designed for use by parents. Violence and pornography have invaded the Internet. Photos and videos of children and young teenagers engaged in sexual acts and various forms of paedophilia are readily available. Reports of children being kidnapped, beaten, raped and murdered abound.

The information and communication technologies have not only changed the rules of the game, they have also moved the playing field. Save our Children, a California based child protection organization, has identified over 8,000 Internet sites dealing with paedophilia. A Japanese wire service reported 500,000 pornographic sites, based in Japan, of which a considerable percentage contain paedophliac images. The danger is not that children will accidentally happen on to theses sites.

Most of the blatantly illegal sites are well hidden to escape detection by the police. The real danger is that other public sites continue to increase in number and to perpetuate paedophilia and the production of pornography all over the world. One such site addressed to 'boy lovers' has links to over 800 other sites - all of them with 'legally acceptable' images of children.

The Internet has in many cases replaced the media of such paedophiliac magazines, films and videos. It is a practical, cheap, convenient and untraceable means for conducting business as well as for trafficking in paedophilia and child pornography. The Internet has also become the principal medium for dialogue about paedophilia and its perpetuation. Fully aware of the need to safeguard freedom of expression, UNESCO nonetheless seeks to make the Internet a safe place for children. It is in this context that the Director-General of UNESCO convened a meeting of experts at UNESCO Headquarters on 18-19 January 1999. More than 400 specialists and institutions, from over 40 countries attended. The participants adopted a Declaration and a Plan of action. UNESCO, as the UN agency with a primary role of catalyzer, was asked to take the lead in 'breaking the silence'. In accordance with its mandate, UNESCO proposed to use its educational, cultural, social and communication expertise to contribute to providing safety nets for children online. This means:

—setting up an electronic clearing house for NGOs, researchers, media, judiciary services and other actors to inform and be informed, to seek advice and resources in total transparency. As there are already several networks in operation, this should be rather an electronic interactive index of child care organizations and networks.

—the creation of two electronic watchtowers. One will act as an online helpline for young children to obtain advice and help. The other is for reporting illegal contents or sites, and will enable quick links to appropriate police forces regardless of the country where the sites are hosted, or the country reporting the crime.

— a polyglot glossary of terms covering all the themes of this meeting.

— generating funds and using this first circle of donor partners from the private sector to create what the Director General has referred to as a strategic group of personalities and leading citizens to lend resonance to the work, to marshal resources, and to state the case of children to the world.

— promoting and supporting the design of handbooks and safety brochures for children, teachers and parents.

Copyright and Neighbouring Rights

Transmission through electronic networks raises problems in the field of copyright and neighbouring rights and it is widely recognized that international co-operation and coordination is necessary to solve them. To explore these problems and be able to advise Member States accordingly, UNESCO organized an International Symposium and three regional Committees of Experts on Communication and Copyright in the Information Society and published a number of articles on these problems in UNESCO's Copyright Bulletin. A crucial role has also been played by the World Intellectual Property Organization (WIPO).

Having organized four international forums and eight Committees of Experts to draw up a draft of two new international instruments to govern the digital transmissions, this organization also convened a Diplomatic Conference of States in December 1996 which adopted a new WIPO Copyright Treaty (WCT) and WIPO Performances and Phonograms Treaty (WPPT). The solution proposed by these treaties was to extend the existing right of 'communication to the public' (the term 'public' was initially interpreted as referring to an undetermined number of people) to digital networks transmission (which may be considered as communication to private persons/subscribers) since the latter make the protected subject matters available to the public 'in such a way that members of the public may access from a place and at a time individually chosen by them'. The treaties also aim to provide additional protection for copyright owners in the digital environment by sanctioning the abuse of technological copyright protection measures, such as hardware or software locks or other encryption mechanisms. Sanctions are also provided against any deliberate tampering with 'rights management information', the ownership data which may accompany digital works.

Largely as a result of argument from African countries at the 1996 Diplomatic Conference, these measures do not restrict the existing cases of 'fair use' or of limitation of and exception from this protection. The new treaties, and their policy background, were discussed in UNESCO's 1997 World Communications Report and in UNESCO's 1998 World Culture Report. It remains to be seen whether adequate legislation is enacted in member countries in the near future. The challenge for policy makers in this field has been the preservation of an appropriate balance between the rights of owners, and the public interest in the free circulation of information. There has been criticism, particularly from developing countries, that enhanced copyright protection inhibits equitable participation in the information society because it further increases the cost of accessing content and applications.

International copyright agreements do not conflict with the more general principle of freedom of expression, which is guaranteed in the Universal Declaration of Human Rights, by article 8 of the European Convention on Human Rights and Fundamental Freedoms and in relevant conventions. A major achievement of the 1996 WIPO Diplomatic Conference in Geneva was the recognition in the preamble to the treaties of the importance of this balance. Copyright law is not merely a legal means to protect the rights of copyright owners: it is directly concerned with the wider goals of enhancing education, science and culture.

Ownership data

Copyright laws around the world have been designed to protect original intellectual works, although the definition of what constitutes originality in this context varies considerably across jurisdictions. Beyond the problem of protecting creative works, however, there are also major policy issues concerning the ownership of factual information or data, such as environmental information, which in itself is usually unprotected by copyright. The new information economy means that what was once a recondite legal question is now a pressing policy issue at an international level.

Information once freely exchanged between countries and organizations is now increasingly seen in a commercial light, with serious consequences for those smaller countries dependent on information - such as meteorological data - which has been gathered by others. This is particularly the case where countries have privatized the public sector organizations that used to collect and distribute information in the past.

Governments around the world are grappling with the question of who should own data and what rules should govern public access and use. The new global networks have made data more valuable than ever before. The market for information has increased enormously as expensive proprietary databases have been replaced by ubiquitous public standards. But these same public networks are also seen as a threat to the data that they carry. In Europe and the United States, database publishers claim that they are now at greater risk of data piracy and attacks from hackers.

Tough new laws are required to protect existing databases, and provide sufficient incentives for the industry to grow. They highlight the vulnerability of data, pointing to the ease with which large quantities of digital information can be copied and redistributed internationally. A database worth millions of dollars, they say, can now be pirated and resold at minimal cost over the Internet. After various discussions held at the international level, agreement has been reached that the provisions of the Berne Convention dealing with copyright protection of compilations of various materials, originally relating to compilations in printed form, should also cover the compilations in electronic form, i.e. databases. The criteria for the protection should be the same as for the compilations in printed form: they are protected by copyright only if by reason of selection or arrangement of their contents they constitute intellectual creations. This was further expressly confirmed under the Agreement on Trade Related Aspects of Intellectual Property Rights (TRIP) adopted in 1995 under the aegis of the former GATT and at present annexed to the World Trade Organization Treaty, and the above mentioned WIPO Copyright Treaty and WIPO Performances and Phonograms Treaty adopted in 1996.

According to these two new international instruments, the exploitation of compilations/databases in digital environment is subject to the copyright owner's authorization in virtue of his/her right of communication to the public. Before the adoption of the treaties the notion 'public' related only to an undetermined number of people.

Although in the digital environment exploitation of the contents is made by individual subscribers, i.e. private persons, digital transmissions were considered to be the equivalent of communication to the public, since the contents are made available to members of the public who may access to the protected subject matter 'from a place and at a time individually chosen by them'.

As in the case of original intellectual works, not only the entire compilations/databases, but also their substantial parts cannot be used without the authorization of the copyright owner. The latter will be determined under national copyrightlaws. However, the treaties failed to resolve the extremely important question of whether the traditional 'fair use' cases or limitations of copyright protection should apply in the digital context. The above solution only partially resolved the problem.

Producers of unstructured databases, those relating to remote sensing for example, which do not correspond to the copyright criteria of 'compilations' also insist on their protection under intellectual property laws to better protect their investment and ensure development of the market. In this respect there were three closely-related proposals to deal with this problem, from the European Union, the United States, and the World Intellectual Property Organization (WIPO).

Europe has progressed the furthest, with a Directive that was largely implemented in member countries by the beginning of 1998. Apart from the provision dealing with the copyright protection of structured compilations/ databases it also provides for *sui generis* protection for those databases which do not correspond to copyright criteria of compilations, but where 'there has been qualitatively and/or quantitatively a substantial investment in their obtaining, verification or presentation of their content'. Owners of such databases are granted the right 'to prevent extraction and/or reutilization of the whole or of a substantial part' of the contents of the database.

In the United States, the initial proposal was strongly opposed by the scientific communities which considered it as limiting the access to and dissemination of scientific information. Compromise legislation on the matter providing for minimal, simpler and more transparent protection is currently being debated in Congress. The problem remains on the agenda of WIPO and has been discussed in a number of their meetings.

The prevailing opinion of the participants in these meetings, including a representative of UNESCO, was that some kind of protection should be granted to the 'non-original' databases to protect the economic interests of their developers. However, the protection should not hamper the specific interests of scientific and educational circles working for the benefit of the society at large and interested in free access, exchange and dissemination of information. In this respect, UNESCO also suggested that a clear distinction be made between the databases produced with public funds and those produced by private enterprises.

The former must be freely accessible to all users, excluding only their exploitation for commercial purposes, and therefore the rules for their protection should not be derived from the logic of competitive exploitation relevant only to databases financed from private funds. At the last meeting held in November 1998, the Permanent Committee asked the International Bureau of WIPO to organize, before it meets in May 1999, regional consultations on the problems, update its documents on national solutions and approaches and prepare a study on the economic and scientific import of the protection of databases for the developing and least developed countries.

Therefore, the problem is likely to be discussed for some time, and no new international treaty on this subject should be expected in the near future. Much will depend on the solution to be adopted in the United States which tends towards the creation of a new kind of intellectual property right, specifically tailored for developers and publishers of databases founded on the notion of 'substantial investment' in the production of a data-base.

It remains to be seen whether this solution is sufficiently flexible with regard to the public interest and 'fair use' cases to strike a balance between the private interests of producers of databases and the interests of the scientific and educational communities in the free circulation of ideas and information.

The new database rules should not have the potential to restrict the scope of fair use or free use. The 1996 European Directive provides for sui generis protection similar to that established under the Berne Convention. Librarians, scientists and educators have expressed concern at both national and international levels that any proposed new database rules should not significantly inhibit researchers seeking to reuse and combine data for publication or for research, or educators wishing to use portions of data sets for instructional purposes.

The new rules are being prepared at a time of increasing fiscal pressure on educational and research institutions in many countries. Governments around the world increasingly look to these bodies to adopt a more commercial approach. The new information technologies provide them with an infrastructure for commercialized data services.

Bibliography

Bjorn-Anderson, N. and Numford, E. (eds)., *Information Society*, North-Holland, 1982.

Brindley, L.J. (ed.), 'The electronic campus: an information strategy', *Library and information research report 73*, London, British Library, 1989.

Coates Joseph F., "The Future of Computer Data Security", *Vital Speeches of the Day*, February 15, 1982.

Computer-Based National Information Systems: Technology and Public Policy Issues Office of Technology Assessment, US Congress, Washington, DC, 1981.

Davis Ruth M., "Computers and Electronics for Individual Services", *Science*, February 12, 1982.

Earl, Michael. *Management Strategies for Information Technology*, Prentice Hall, 1989.

Frieden, R. 1996. *International Telecommunications Handbook*. Northwood, Mass., Artech House. 419 pp.

Gorea. 1995. "Infrastructure for the Global Village". *Scientific American*, pp. 156–9.

Hawkridge David, *New Information Technology in Education*, Croom Helm, London, 1983.

Hogan, M. 1998. "The PC of Tomorrow". *PC World*, January, pp. 132–42.

Kahin B., Nesson , C. (eds.). 1997. *Borders in Cyberspace*. MIT Press, Cambridge, Massachusetts.

Kobayashi, K. 1986. *Computers and Communications. (A vision of C&C)*. Cambridge, Mass., MIT Press. 190 pp.

Rabb, C. D. 1997. Privacy, Democracy, Information. In: B. D. Loader (ed.), *The Governance of Cyberspace*. London, Routledge.

Simons G. L., *Privacy in the Computer Age* NCC, Manchester, England, 1982.

Smith, Christine H. (ed.), *Open Systems Interconnection: the Communications Technology of the 1990s*, London, KG Saur, 1988.

Weizenbaum, Joseph, *Computer Power and Human Reason*, W. H. Freeman, 1976.

Whisler, Thomas, *The Impact of Computer on Organisation*, Praeger, 1970.

Wood Michael, *Introducing Computer Insecurity* NCC, Manchester, England and John Wiley, New York, 1983.

UNESCO. 1997. The World Information Report. Paris, UNESCO.

Index